In Confidence

Talking Frankly about Fame and Fortune

In Confidence

Talking Frankly about Fame and Fortune

Laurie Taylor
with Sally Feldman

Winchester, UK
Washington, USA

First published by Zero Books, 2014
Zero Books is an imprint of John Hunt Publishing Ltd., Laurel House, Station Approach,
Alresford, Hants, SO24 9JH, UK
office1@jhpbooks.net
www.johnhuntpublishing.com
www.zero-books.net

For distributor details and how to order please visit the 'Ordering' section on our website.

Text copyright: Laurie Taylor and Sally Feldman 2013

ISBN: 978 1 78279 767 8

A CIP catalogue record for this book is available from the British Library.

Design: Stuart Davies
www.stuartdaviesart.com

Cover photograph: Timothy Anderson

Printed and bound by CPI Group (UK) Ltd, Croydon, CR0 4YY

We operate a distinctive and ethical publishing philosophy in all
areas of our business, from our global network of authors to
production and worldwide distribution.

CONTENTS

Acknowledgements

Although this book is written in the first person, it owes a huge debt to the intelligence, wit, literacy and sheer endurance of my collaborator and wife, Sally Feldman.

I must also give great credit to Victor Lewis-Smith, who not only devised the TV series but, as head of the production company, Associated Rediffusion, also presided over its making with imagination, sensitivity and the occasional well-timed blast of malevolent humour.

But my primary acknowledgement has to be to the director of *In Confidence*, Roger Pomphrey, who died in January 2014, shortly after the completion of the final series.

In Confidence depended a great deal upon the establishment of a rapid rapport between myself and my celebrity guests. Not an easy thing to achieve in a barn of a studio bristling with lights and equipment. But Roger worked with such quiet effectiveness that I could always handle my part of the proceedings without ever worrying about the complex technical business going on around me.

Roger did more than this. His directorial creativity, his special gift for reading and understanding and framing faces, added an extra artistic dimension to the final programmes. He is sorely missed by all those who knew and worked with him.

Introduction

This book is based on the extended interviews I conducted between 2009 and 2013 for the Sky Arts TV series *In Confidence*.

In all, five series were commissioned, allowing me to enjoy conversations with 60 well-known people from the worlds of literature, music, art, politics and popular entertainment. It was an extraordinarily varied experience. One week I would be listening to Nigel Kennedy describing the manner in which Stéphane Grappelli changed his view of musical performing, while only a week later I might be questioning Tracey Emin about the role of self-revelation in art, or laughing at David Starkey's exuberant account of "coming out" on Hampstead Heath.

As one series gave way to another I became increasingly aware of the many convergences and contradictions between what my guests had to say about their childhood dreams and disappointments, their sources of inspiration, their fears of failure and their ways of handling fame and celebrity.

It was fascinating enough, for example, to learn from my interview that the singer and songwriter Lily Allen dealt with fame by regarding the "Lily Allen" who appeared on stage as almost a separate being, an artfully assembled creation. But this became even more intriguing when contrasted with John Lydon's vehement insistence that there was nothing whatsoever posed about his stage appearance as Johnny Rotten. His image was himself. There was no separate identity. You got what you saw. Take it or leave it.

In much the same manner, while it was certainly interesting enough to discover Stephen Fry's ambivalence about his fame, his repetitive concern that it was a result of media ubiquity rather than an appreciation of his actual talent, this gained in purchase when contrasted with Tom Baker's readiness to embrace the attention of his fans, his happy acceptance of their "adoration".

But this book has provided one other opportunity. In the last 50 years, the study of celebrity that is usually seen as building upon Daniel Boorstin's much-quoted 1961 assertion that "the celebrity is a person who is well-known for their well-knownness" has become almost an academic discipline in its own right. It not only considers how celebrities are produced and maintained but also how they are consumed by the public, and how the cult of celebrity may, since the decline of organised religion, have become one of the new ways of promoting social meaning and solidarity. We may no longer all share in the dramas and melodramas of *Coronation Street* as we did in the earlier days of TV but we are participants, however unwillingly, in debates about the integrity of Princess Diana's tears or the aesthetic merits of Jeremy Paxman's beard.

It is almost an article of faith among such professional scholars that celebrity in today's world is an attribution and not an inherent quality. Alan Ayckbourn and E. L. Doctorow and Michael Frayn might indeed share the belief that they are not "celebrities" when compared to such other figures in this book as Nigel Kennedy or Sheila Hancock or Uri Geller, but analysts are unwilling to allow them off the hook. David Giles, in *Illusions of Immortality*, puts it this way: "The brutal reality of the modern age is that all famous people are treated like celebrities by the mass media whether they be a great political figure, a worthy campaigner, an artist 'touched by genius', a serial killer or Maureen of *Driving School* . . . the newspapers and TV programs responsible for their publicity do not draw any meaningful distinction between *how* they are publicised."

Sociologists bearing theories are dangerous beasts and I have no doubt that some of the interpretations I've placed upon some of my interviewees' remarks are contentious. But as all the interviews in the *In Confidence* programmes depended, without exception, upon the cut and thrust of mutual conversation rather upon the mere eliciting of anecdotes, I can argue that what follows maintains that discursive tradition even when my voice is the only one to be heard.

Part One

Welcome to the Show

Chapter One

Tell Me About It

Many years before the BBC, in common with other major organisations, decided that training was something to be capitalised as Training and carried out by Professional Trainers rather than passed on like a craft from person to person, there was, in circulation around Broadcasting House, a five-minute tape recording that served as a *vade mecum* on what not to do in a radio interview.

The recording, originally made in 1955, features a very upper-class BBC female presenter interviewing a citizen of Tunbridge Wells who is about to celebrate his 103rd birthday.

"Well now, Mr Crunwell," she begins in her cut-glass accent. "You tell me about Tunbridge Wells."

Mr Crunwell is clearly at a loss. "I don't know anything about it," he says in his broad local accent. "Only that it's Tunbridge Wells."

Not a promising start. But the lady from the BBC persists. What changes have have there been to Tunbridge Wells over the many years in which Mr Crunwell has resided there? What's the nicest thing about Tunbridge Wells?

"I don't know," says Mr Crunwell.

"Don't you know anything nice about it?"

"No, I know nothing about Tunbridge Wells."

At this point in the recording, Mr Crunwell seems to sense that something more is required of him.

"I don't know what you want me to say but if I can say anything to please you . . ."

I was happy enough at the time to join in the general office laughter at the expense of the lady interviewer. How could anyone be so insensitive to context? How could anyone fail to recognise that there was a real charm about the old man's refusal to respond to her checklist of questions? But then I played the tape again and realised that it was a record of something rather more profound than a badly handled interview.

It wasn't that the aged resident of Tunbridge Wells was being especially unresponsive or even that the interviewer was being especially insensitive. The problem was the interview itself. Mr Crunwell simply couldn't understand why someone he didn't know from Eve was standing in front of him with a microphone and asking questions. He hadn't yet learned how to play one of the essential roles in the new age of radio and TV. He hadn't yet learned how to be an interviewee.

Today, no one is at all surprised to be greeted in the high street by smiling interviewers bearing microphones. Today no one finds anything unusual in a complete stranger eliciting our opinions on and emotional responses to matters as diverse as a new toothpaste flavour and the latest crisis in the Middle East. Radio and TV would be quite empty without such instant opinions. ("Let's do a vox pop," goes up the cry in TV and radio production offices whenever it is felt that a programme needs "a common touch".)

The interview is no longer one mode of organising media talk; it is the form that dominates all others. From early morning to late at night, packs of presenters are busy soliciting hard facts and debatable opinions and emotional confessions from an almost endless stream of interviewees. No wonder that such a ubiquitous way of managing talk should become subject to ridicule and parody. There were some episodes of *Monty Python's Flying Circus* in the early '70s in which the only comic device seemed to be the eccentric interview.

But while the Python team, along with The Two Ronnies and Fry and Laurie and Bird and Fortune, exploited every possible comic aspect of the media interview – the seating arrangements, the pomposity of experts, the incoherence of footballers, the narcissism of actors and the evasiveness of politicians – there were others who sought to raise its status and increase its seriousness.

It was no doubt Michael Parkinson's background in journalism that informed his determination to make his interview programme into something that was more informative, more conversational, than the conventional chat show. Not only would the guest list for *Parkinson* include people who had established their reputations outside the narrow confines of showbiz but also there would be a conscious attempt to prompt a conversation rather than merely provide cues on which the interviewee could hang a promotion. Although the presenter would still have cue cards, the removal of his desk (at the time a standard feature of American chat shows) was seen as another way of democratising the format.

But what also made Michael Parkinson stand out from the pack was his obvious involvement with his guests. As Simon Hattenstone recently observed in *The Guardian*, "He brought such enthusiasm to the job – crying with laughter at Tommy Cooper, in awe of polymath Jacob Bronowski, mesmerised by Ali, fatherly to David Beckham, agog at the world's most beautiful women ... As he scratched away at himself, or picked his nose when particularly absorbed, he really did seem to forget he was on TV."

All was well as long as Parkinson retained that enthusiasm, as long as we could believe that he was so genuinely impressed by his guests that he had no wish to promote his own status. While it's true that even in the early days those guests were usually hoping to plug a forthcoming book or play, at that time the publicity machine was not so finely tuned. An interview with Parkinson was not seen merely as an opportunity to plug. It was also an occasion to talk with varying degrees of honesty about one's life and times and present and past loves.

There were two developments that undermined the appeal of this admirable interview programme. The first was biographical.

In the early days Parkinson had been meeting his real heroes, the unattainable stars of his childhood and adolescence. Parkinson and his viewers could share his excitement. This was the first time they had ever seen stars like Ingrid Bergman and Bette Davis and Robert Redford and James Stewart and Robert Mitchum away from the big screen and in the relative domesticity and scale of a TV studio. But the increasing importance of TV threw up a whole new class of celebrities who lacked the aura of their filmic predecessors. They might have been well known but Parkinson could rarely even simulate the degree of interest in their goings-on that came quite naturally to him when he was faced by his real heroes.

As the guests became more mundane, the publicity machines became more polished. Producers who wished to feature celebrities on their chat shows were told that they could only obtain their services if they guaranteed a specified amount of time, a specified number of clips, to the star's latest product. No guarantee, no appearance. There were plenty of other chat shows around that would be more obliging. Whereas in earlier times the plug could often be disregarded, it now became the *raison d'être* for the interview, a point of reference that constantly earthed the rest of the conversation.

The Parkinson show crumbled under the impact of these developments. While the ever more blatant plugging made it impossible to maintain the genial fiction that the guests were there because they relished the chance of a chat with Parkie, the decline in the quality of the interviewees meant that it was often difficult to believe in the presenter's declared pleasure at having them there in the first place. There was something slightly sad about watching the man who had so unambiguously (and so believably) worshipped Muhammad Ali endeavouring to work up anything approaching a similar degree of enthusiasm for Sharon Osbourne.

It was this very attenuation of the concept of celebrity that paradoxically allowed for the rise of the "celebrity presenter". Parkinson had indeed become well known through his visual association with his guests, but now presenters acquired their fame by using their guests as resources to develop their own star status. Guests were no longer to be treated with a Parkinsonian awe or respect but were expected to serve as butts for the presenter's gags. Parkinson ruefully characterised the development as "the lunatics taking over the asylum".

This shift of emphasis also meant that the type of extended seriousness that often found a place in the early Parkinson shows would now give way in the average chat show to little more than a continuous attempt to create a laugh, manufacture a *double entendre* ("Ooh, what have I just said?") or prompt an embarrassing story. I once asked the BBC's one-time religious correspondent Gerald Priestland about his attitude to Russell Harty's matey style of radio and TV interviewing. "I have nothing against Harty," said Priestland. "But I have no wish at all to get down on all fours and play with him." It's a characterisation I remember when I'm watching even such an accomplished performer as Graham Norton gamely trying to make his guests share his happy silliness. As Parkinson himself has observed, "People like Graham Norton and Jonathan Ross don't do talk shows. They are comedy shows, which they are very good at, but the guests are foils for their humour." He took much the same perspective on the best known of American chat-show hosts: "Letterman, Leno and Carson couldn't interview their way out of a paper bag, but they are wonderful stand-up comics."

It's easy to understand Parkinson's concern about the deterioration of the celebrity interview. He was, after all, originally inspired by watching the famous 1959–62 series *Face to Face* in which John Freeman interviewed a wide selection of famous guests ranging from psychoanalyst Carl Gustav Jung to pop star Adam Faith. What distinguished this series from so many other talk shows was the absence of Freeman himself. All that viewers were allowed was the occasional shot of the back of his head. As Parkinson commented, "He was the most famous face in Britain, yet you never saw his face. The camera was always on the person he was talking to, yet he became hugely famous."

Face to Face insisted upon seriousness. Its signature tune was an excerpt from the overture to one of Berlioz's uncompleted operas and each episode was introduced by a specially commissioned portrait of the guest by artist Feliks Topolski. And although it is now best remembered for its emotional moments (Gilbert Harding's sadness about the death of his mother and Tony Hancock's admissions of self-doubt that were later to be seen as anticipating his suicide) it was remorselessly intelligent. Rather than prompting his subjects to tell stories about themselves, to recall anecdotes, Freeman asked short leading questions. Indeed, at times, the programme can now sound more like a job interview than an analytic session. Here, for example, is a random sample of the questions from that famous Hancock interview.

"Being funny is part of the business of finding out about life. Is that right?"

"What is there about you that makes people laugh? You must have some idea."

"What would you like to most reform about the world if you had a chance?"

"Can you recall a moment in life when your God failed you?"

"Do you find yourself answerable in your moral judgement to anyone but yourself?"

So while it is true that Harding looked tearful (but never cried) and Hancock revealed a disturbing degree of self-doubt, it's now at least arguable that what really disconcerted some of the guests was not so much the subtlety of the actual questioning as the novelty (at that time) of being invited to speak publicly about their feelings. Nowadays celebrities are not so readily disturbed or undermined. They have their "confessions" well prepared in advance.

It was not until 1982 and the first broadcast on BBC Radio 4 of *In the Psychiatrist's Chair* that psychological techniques were explicitly brought to bear upon the celebrity interview. The programme's presenter Anthony Clare was a practising psychiatrist and a broadcasting colleague of mine on the Radio 4 chat show *Stop the Week*. It was this association that allowed me to listen in on the vigorous and long-running debate between Clare and his producer Michael Ember about the appropriateness of using the word "psychiatrist" in its title. For although Clare was committed to probing the psychological character of his celebrity guests, to considering the influence upon them of their childhood and their parenting, he was of the opinion that to call this "psychiatric" was to do a disservice to the manner in which he conducted interviews with the patients in his care. He was indeed a psychiatrist but these were not psychiatric interviews.

But the title stayed and, although there were mutterings from the psychiatric profession, Clare's capacity to disconcert his guests, to cause Bob Monkhouse and Paddy Ashdown to break down in tears as they talked about their parents, not only ensured a long run for the series but made Clare himself the respectable and friendly face of British psychiatry.

What was so odd, however, about Clare's role in the programme was that, although he frequently used childhood experiences as a way into the character of the celebrity before him, he himself had little time for Freudian analysis. Indeed he once told me that it was his interviewees' belief in the importance of childhood experiences that led them to break up when the subject was raised rather than the facts of these experiences.

But however much I pressed him on the matter I was never able to persuade Clare to confirm or deny the popular rumour inside Broadcasting House that at least some of the potency ascribed to his interviewing was the result of a little legerdemain with the pause button. All the programmes were recorded and quite heavily edited. This meant that the producer could not only cut out dull passages but, so it was alleged, give extra psychological weight to certain moments by artificially lengthening the pause between Clare's question and the guest's answer. "Did you love your mother?" Long pause. "Yes, I did." Take out that pause and one's left with nothing but banality.

Although knowing and liking Anthony Clare had made me particularly intrigued with his interview series, my enduring interest in interviewing itself, whether conducted by the forensic intellectual John Freeman, the super-fan Michael Parkinson or the cheerily self-serving Graham Norton, arose quite simply from my day job. As a sociologist I spend a great deal of time describing and analysing successful pieces of ethnography in which the researcher has been required to extract information from difficult and recalcitrant subjects. My heroes are the social scientists who often spend years in the field in order to obtain access to the worlds of drug takers or prostitutes or football hooligans or the members of delinquent gangs.

It was a fortunate accident that gave me a chance to enter a particularly secret subculture: the world of professional crime. Way back in the late '60s when I first joined York University, I accepted an invitation to give lectures in sociology to a group of inmates in Durham Prison. To the surprise of myself and my fellow lecturer, Stan Cohen, most of the members of our class turned out to be professional criminals whose exploits had earned them very long sentences: they included John McVicar, the bank robber, Bruce Reynolds from the Great Train Robbery, the notorious gang leader Charlie Richardson and a couple of former members of the Kray Brothers' organisation.

I became particularly friendly with McVicar, who developed a real interest in sociology and eventually obtained a degree in the subject. It was a friendship that I was anxious to continue when he was eventually released from prison in the early '80s. Perhaps, I suggested, we could write about professional crime.

For although there was no shortage of books about criminals, nearly all of them were based upon interviews with imprisoned villains and delinquents. There weren't any about the criminals who didn't get caught, the professionals who lived a life of crime. John had extraordinary access to such working criminals. If he'd effect a few introductions to such people – drug dealers, confidence men, armed robbers, gangsters – then I could set up my tape-recorder and begin interviewing.

It seemed a simple proposition but John was wary. And I soon found out why. One of the first working criminals he took me to meet was Geoff, a professional conman who made a very good living out of forging signatures on stolen traveller's cheques and credit cards. He was happy enough to meet me in his flat but everything changed when I switched on my tape-recorder and asked him the first question. It was a moment that took me right back to Mr Crunwell and Tunbridge Wells. For Geoff's instant response to my first question demonstrated that we came from very different worlds.

"Well, Geoff, thanks for agreeing to talk to me," I said. "Now, how long have you been a professional criminal?" Geoff promptly stood up. "Look, Laurie. I'll tell you this. You'll have to go a bit slower than that. I mean I hear a question . . . I hear a fucking question like, 'Well, Geoff', or 'Now, Geoff', and I'm away. I mean I associate questions with trouble. That's right, isn't it, John?" John nodded. "I associate questions with guilty pleas. And that's something I never do. Nothing to say. Nothing to say. Nothing to say. Right down the sheet. That's my way. I don't do questions."

This wasn't a solitary reaction. As I quickly learned, nobody who made a living out of crime was happy with questions. They not only didn't like my questions, they didn't ask each other questions. Nobody asked where anybody had been to or was going to. Nobody, certainly, asked what anybody was feeling or thinking.

John McVicar had only one sentence of advice. As we sat in my flat that evening drinking the thick dark tea that he'd come to favour during his years in the security wing because of the caffeine kick it provided, he gave me one of his now familiar "told-you-so" looks. "I'm not taking you to see another villain," he said emphatically, "until you promise to stop posing around like Michael Parkinson."

All these thoughts about interviewing came to mind on the day back in 2009 when Sky Arts offered me a chance to develop a series of interview programmes.

I quickly decided on one omission. Myself. I was well aware that what gave John Freeman's *Face to Face* its reputation was not just the high quality of the guests or the intelligence of the questioning. It was the manner in which those guests always held centre stage because of the almost total invisibility of the presenter.

But even if *In Confidence* was going to look rather like *Face to Face*, right from the start I wanted to make one very significant change. Although Freeman obtained quite dramatic results from his forensic style of questioning, it was difficult to imagine this being half so effective in an era in which celebrities had become so sophisticated at handling their moments of "self-revelation". Could one really imagine that someone like Damien Hirst or David Schwimmer would suddenly admit to deep inner feelings when they were straightforwardly asked about their life and loves? Nowadays, I reasoned, any such questions could at best only prompt well-remembered and well-rehearsed anecdotes. I had another form of talk in mind: the conversation. This had often been promised in other media shows but rarely achieved. Hosts might chatter on about one topic for a few minutes with their guest but then either the pressure of time or the fear of generating boredom invariably meant that they turned to the next question on their cue sheet.

Part of my enthusiasm for conversation was based on the

many years I spent on the Radio 4 programme *Stop the Week*. Although much of the talk was about such mundane matters as the best place to cut one's toenails (Ann Leslie insisted upon the bath) or the character of a person who asks for a knife and fork in a Chinese restaurant, the chairman Robert Robinson always had a model in his head of what a good conversation should sound like. It should be free-wheeling, without any sort of goal in mind. It should involve cut and thrust and eager turn-taking. It should, like a good game of tennis, engender rallies in which none of the participants controlled the next point in the game. (He used to rail against the occasional guest on the programme who "could not hit the ball back" or kept on missing "the simplest of lobs".)

This was never an elitist position. Good conversationalists could be found anywhere. In this respect he certainly agreed with his idol, Doctor Johnson, that "the pleasure which men are able to give in conversation, holds no stated proportion to their knowledge or their virtue." In any good conversation, Robinson once observed, "we are on stage, but in the most pleasing of roles, ourselves as we would be thought to be! We suspend the purely utilitarian functions in favour of performance."

Few people have captured this aspect of conversation as well as Theodore Zeldin. In his book *Conversation: How Talk Can Change Your Life* he provides this characterisation of its unpredictable quality: "Conversation is a meeting of minds with different memories and habits. When minds meet they don't just exchange facts: they transform them, reshape them, draw different implications from them, engage in new trains of thought. Conversation doesn't just reshuffle the cards: it creates new cards."

But there was one big problem. In the Sky Arts programmes I was going to be dealing with people who had had a long experience of being interviewed and would, in the name of an easy life, probably prefer that form of talk. They would have plenty of biographical anecdotes at hand, plenty of accounts of their successes and relative failures, plenty of ways of avoiding any chatter that got too close to the bone.

This meant that the preparation could not be entrusted to a young researcher with a fat bundle of cuttings. Something more was needed. And at this point I came up with the notion of conversational themes. Instead of using the biographical material merely to prompt reminiscence I used it to generate philosophical dilemmas. So, in conversation with Michael Frayn, my questions would not only be about the specific character of his father but about the problems that might afflict a novelist who had drawn upon his childhood in his fictional work and now needed to revisit that childhood in order to construct a "truthful" family biography.

In much the same way I was happy to ask Lily Allen about the absurdities of being famous because I knew that after she'd stressed her ordinariness I could then suggest that such self-deprecation was now the most common way for celebrities to handle their fame. What was wrong, I would ask, about allowing yourself to be famous?

So this book is not simply a collection of interviews with my favourite people. It is also, I trust, a kind of philosophical journey in which a series of celebrities tackle a variety of paradoxes and contradictions that have been thrown up by their art or their technique or their childhood or their fame.

Chapter Two

Celebrity Squares

Tom Baker – Stephen Fry – David Starkey – Lily Allen – Uri Geller

Back in the mid-1970s I presented a programme on Granada TV with the rather extravagant title *The Great British Drink Test*. Its intention was to disturb viewers with some hard facts about the real amounts of drink they consumed in an average evening. On the face of it a noble enough endeavour. But I can well remember that during the making of the programme we consistently cheated by repeatedly raising the limit for safe drinking so that it kept most of the production staff comfortably clear of the "dangerous" category. Two pints of beer rapidly became four while three modest glasses of wine morphed into a whole bottle. But this statistical legerdemain was a minor fault compared with my ineptitude as a popular science presenter. When I dared to glance at the film recently I could not quite decide what was the most unfortunate aspect of my presentation: the ill-fitting suit or the mock matiness or the silly walk or the plonking attempts at humour?

When I finally crawled back to the university department where I earned my proper salary, there was silence about my screen alter ego. Perhaps no one had seen it. Perhaps everyone had seen it and decided to keep quiet. But then one day as I walked across campus to a lecture hall I was halted by the university's senior professor of philosophy. "Caught that programme the other night," he said with the tone of a man who'd inadvertently trodden in something unpleasant. "You know, you're getting to be a bit of a celebrity." That was all. But his face told me that he could think of no more ignominious fate.

At the time I fretted about the manner in which the remark

sidestepped any reference to the content of my programme. But when I thought about it later, it seemed to capture something critical about the nature of celebrity. It suggested that "celebrity" was a relative term: one could be a "bit of a celebrity" rather than the fully-fledged thing. But it also simultaneously implied that celebrity was something unfortunate that could all too readily creep up on one, like athlete's foot.

This view of celebrity as an almost wholly negative category owes a great deal to the sociologist Daniel Boorstin. For although his famous declaration in the early 1960s that "the celebrity is a person who is well-known for their well-knownness" continues to provide a useful weapon for those who want to rail against our present celebrity-obsessed culture, it needs to be seen in context. Boorstin was not merely trying to put celebrities in their place; he was also complaining that their ubiquity was evidence of the lack of authenticity that he believed characterised contemporary American culture.

But this is an all too familiar way of denigrating the new. Those who find themselves out of tune with modern popular music or film or TV readily resort to the notion of the authentic when they want to champion or glorify the achievements of the past. This is how Graham Turner puts it in *Understanding Celebrity*: "Each new shift in fashion is offered as the end of civilisation as we know it, with the real motivation being an elitist distaste for the demotic or populist dimension of mass cultural practices."

It is not too surprising, then, to find that Boorstin doesn't merely wish to document the vacuity of contemporary celebrity but also wants to return to a time when the word had proper authentic meaning, a time when people were well known not for being well-known but because they could boast of some specific achievement. These "truly heroic" figures were distinguished by "the great simple virtues of their character".

Although Boorstin's analysis can now be viewed as a

somewhat traditional way of denigrating contemporary popular culture and even romanticising the past, his contrast between real virtue and mere celebrity was still one that exercised a great many of my *In Confidence* guests. Every one of them had been regularly lauded (and often lavishly rewarded) for their distinctive achievements, but it was rare for them to accept or embrace such popular acclaim as wholly or even partially deserved. Anything that smacked of the type of fan worship that was accorded to the mere celebrity was to be firmly detached from proper critical opinion. Even the literary figures I interviewed were aware that part of their well-knownness derived not from the intrinsic merits of their work but from the workings of the publicity machines that ensured their names were recognised and from the attention of fans who in so many respects resembled the fans of any other celebrity. As Joe Moran writes in *Understanding Celebrity*, the "fact that literary fans might like to think of themselves as pursuing an interest in an artist rather than a celebrity" is really only an attempt to locate themselves "on a slightly higher plane of cultural consumption".

How did my interviewees handle these dilemmas? How much did they wish to separate what they believed to be their real "heroic" character from their celebrity-tainted public image? How did they react to those "fans" who persistently appeared to be considerably more interested in who they were, in the fact of their fame, than in what they did?

In these respects nobody intrigued me quite so much as the actor Tom Baker, who many critics and fans still regard as the quintessential Doctor Who. Tom was a year below me at the Rose Bruford College of Speech and Drama in Sidcup, Kent, and during our time together we became friends. It was not, however, a love of drama or acting that drew us together but the shared sense of extreme malaise induced by life at the college. Nowadays I understand that Rose Bruford College has a fine reputation, but back in the late '50s and early '60s it seemed to be largely staffed by teachers who believed that speaking Received Pronunciation, being able to simulate both Evil and Good in a mime class, knowing how to deliver an Elizabethan bow and remembering one's stage right from one's stage left were the essential prerequisites for a successful career on the boards. Whereas Tom and I were respectively working-class and lower-middle-class boys from Liverpool, most of the rest of the students were middle-class girls from the southern counties who were rather less inspired by the idea of inhabiting the role of Hedda Gabler than by coming out as a debutante.

After college, Tom had difficulty finding any acting work, while I took a psychology degree in the evenings at Birkbeck College and eventually became a sociology lecturer at York. We met up again when he briefly appeared at the York Theatre Royal playing the Michael Caine role in *Educating Rita*, and we resolved to keep in touch. The first opportunity came a few months later when he was successfully auditioned for the role of Doctor Who and I was informed by the University Council that I'd been made a full professor. "Bloody hell, Tom," said my telegram. "A doctorate and a chair in the same week! Time to celebrate."

Tom's fine knowing performance as Doctor Who, coupled with his forays into children's literature and his aptitude for voice-overs (which reached a sort of apotheosis in the surreal links he provided for *Little Britain*), meant that he became easily the most famous graduate of Rose Bruford College even if his success was almost entirely founded on those booming extravagant aspects of his personality that the acting tutors had so earnestly sought to eradicate.

So when I interviewed him for *In Confidence* I was intrigued to know what he made now of his rise to stardom. "Are you happy being a celebrity?" I asked. "Happy to have to attend so many *Doctor Who* conventions and shake so many hands?"

"Well, you know," he told me with undisguised relish. "I'm a sort of god in the science fantasy world. And my fans have become a sort of pilgrims and they don't go to Lourdes or Mecca or Medina or wherever, they come to, say, Camber Sands, to Pontins. When I arrive they handle me and worship me and I congratulate them on their taste and I sign their autographs, very affectionately."

I wasn't too surprised by Tom's frankness about his popularity. I remembered that even in the early days of *Doctor Who* he would deal with fans by being excessively charming. He'd sign autographs and pose for photos with a ready smile. There were a few limits. One night after he'd been excessively badgered in the street, he retired into a bar where he was immediately accosted by a drunk. "Didn't I see you on television the other night?" he slurped. Tom grabbed him by the tie and pulled him forward. "Didn't I see you *watching* television the other night?" he said aggressively.

Was he still happy to be recognised in the street by all and sundry?

"I can't complain really because I always wanted to be loved. And then, as I got more confident I wanted to be adored and now, in the twilight of my life, I have to tell you the good news, now I'm, well – worshipped really."

But how could he be pleased to be adored for merely being a face off the TV? It wasn't as though the fans who wanted to touch and to kiss him were showing their admiration for his acting skills or his intelligence. They were "worshipping" him for his fame.

No, that didn't worry him one jot. He had a handy irreverent analogy. The fans, he told me, "tremble a lot, the way one does with a god. It's a long time since I trembled, but I used to tremble in front of the tabernacle when I was young in Liverpool. Because at that time I was a fan of God. I was devoted to him. It was incredible. Of course, I've forgiven him now, now that I've discovered he doesn't exist."

It's easy enough to dismiss Tom's happy embracing of his

fame as an act, a clever way of handling his celebrity status so that it doesn't impinge upon his real inner being. But that's far from the truth. He simply doesn't believe that he is really a fine actor who has accidentally had that aspect of his character obscured by his celebrity status.

"I don't really rate my acting, but my Doctor Who was entirely Tom. It was just Tom. I wasn't acting it. It just fell into my lap. And I thought, hey, who wants to act? I can be Tom. They're loving Tom."

But although this thought allows him to relish rather than deny or seek to make light of his fame, it doesn't mean that he has any illusions about his own significance.

"I remember one time in Sloane Square where I used to cruise at the height of my fame. I was outside Peter Jones, which was a good place to cruise, and a little old lady, very old, had been a great beauty in her time, said, 'Hello, dear.' And I was used to this and said, 'Hello.' And she said, 'Oh,' and clutched her bosom rather operatically and said, 'I'm so sorry, do I know you, or am I going dotty?' And I said, gently, I said, 'Perhaps you've got grandchildren.' 'Oh, yes', she said, 'you're the man from *Doctor Who*. As soon as I saw you I knew you were special because my titties began to tingle.' And I thought, isn't that marvellous, you know? My mother, who was lovely, could never have said a phrase like that. And I thought perhaps on my gravestone: 'Here lies Tom Baker who made titties tingle.' It about sums up the silliness of telly fame."

Some might suspect the ingenuousness of these declarations. Surely Tom wanted some of the admiration he received to constitute a proper acknowledgment of his talent rather than a recognition of his fame? Wasn't he dissembling somewhat? I doubt it. In other conversations with Tom, I've always been fascinated by his readiness to quote from the writings of his own set of no-nonsense heroes: Saul Bellow, Philip Roth, Christopher Hitchens. These are people who really matter to him, who provide an acerbic contrast to the indulgent self-serving world of showbiz. How could he ever allow himself to think that anything he did had any value compared to the literary output of his superstars?

But whereas Tom seems to have an open-hearted, open-minded, often comical (and, it should be added, thoroughly materialistic) view of his celebrity, matters are far more ambiguous for Stephen Fry. Fry's films and very regular TV appearances ensure that he enjoys much the same kind of instant recognition as Tom Baker. But he seems constantly anxious to distinguish between the sort of recognition that properly acknowledges his literary and acting talents and that which is merely accorded him for being a constant face on our TV screens. His readiness to appear in so many public roles certainly suggests a desire, an almost constant desire, for public appreciation, but he seems to live in a permanent dread of receiving any sort of criticism.

For someone so ubiquitous, so used to the glare of the limelight and the relatively uncritical endorsement of his millions of Twitter followers, he was strangely nervous when he arrived, fashionably late, at our studios. He claimed to be suffering from a headache, was slightly tetchy. After only a few moments he threatened to walk out of the interview, when I simply asked him how he reacted to newspaper reviews. "If you've come here to tell me something that's in a newspaper I will have to leave," he complained, going on to claim that he hadn't read a newspaper in 12 years and was all the better for it. Was this, I wondered, because he feared criticism? Not at all, he retorted. You have to accept that when you're in the public eye you're going to be lambasted from time to time. "When a book comes out and suddenly you're doing events or you're being interviewed or you're trapped by a journalist and you say something mild about the Pope and then suddenly every *Spectator* journalist decides it's fine to call you the Antichrist, you know, and naturally you feel a little beleaguered, to say the least. Believe me, it's a little beleaguering, it isn't a big moan."

Unlike Tom Baker, who has settled for his fame – come to regard it almost as some sort of recognition, however partial or deranged, of his own personality – Stephen Fry appears to be in a constant dialogue with his own celebrity status. It is something that needs to be separated from his real self, an aspect of existence that has to be acknowledged, albeit with some unwillingness, and then adroitly managed.

"Anyone with any modicum of pride is going to have to find a way of coping with it," he told me. "It's unbelievably rude to pretend it isn't there. I am above such things, you know. I certainly don't watch myself on television but if people go, 'Oh, you're always on Dave, how's that?' You know, you say the decent British thing. You say, 'I know. It's ridiculous, I'm so sorry.' Absurd."

Of course one of the ways in which you can try to manage fame is by suggesting that you don't take yourself too seriously, that you have a degree of self-consciousness about everything you do that marks you off from all those other celebrities who believe what they read about themselves, who take themselves too seriously. But as the American historian Christopher Lasch argued so persuasively in *The Culture of Narcissism*, this attempt to demonstrate ironic detachment is also an act, an illusion. Distancing soon becomes a routine in its own right. It also leads nowhere except into further spirals of reflexivity. Look at me looking at me looking at me. It is, in Lasch's wonderful phrase, "the banality of pseudo-self-awareness".

This is a trait that others have observed in Fry's on-screen performances. *Sunday Times* TV critic A. A. Gill astutely captures the manner in which Fry's attempts to elicit the viewer's admiration or appreciation by undermining his own celebrity status can lead to the creation of a wholly unbelievable TV persona. Here is Gill reviewing Fry's performance in *The Bleak*

Old Shop of Stuff, TV's attempt to have some knowing Christmas-time fun with Dickens: "His enormous, perchance bottomless and truly selfless desire to be who you would like him to be has led to a character who, in his voluminous wit and whimsy, his cravenly apologetic self-mockery, has travelled quite some distance from a Stephen Fry his doctor or accountant might recognise."

I don't, of course, quote Gill to Fry. He's already made his attitude towards criticism pretty clear. But I do suggest that some of the weariness he seems to feel about having to cope with his fame might be readily alleviated by cutting down on some of his public appearances.

"I do feel that I'd love to close down for a number of years in some way and just be in the country making pork pies and chutneys and never have to poke my head out of the parapet. It's exhausting knowing that most of the time the phone rings, most of the time there's an email, most of the time there's a letter that someone wants something off you. And it's not off you personally, it's off that rind on you, that's the layer fame can give. They want to touch the hem of the fame, not the hem of the person."

Why then, for example, did he feel the need to make TV commercials? One could readily understand why other, lesser-known celebrities might wish to cash in on their fame while it lasted, but surely someone who was so assured of fame, as well as being so publicly associated with good causes, should think twice before accepting the advertiser's tainted shilling?

Was it simply the money? Not at all. "I will continue to do commercials because they're so enjoyable. Not because of the money because I don't need the money, but because it's really wonderful."

But there's yet another way of handling celebrity. You don't need to hug it to yourself in the manner of Tom Baker or attempt to distance it from the "hem of the person" as Stephen Fry contends. You can also cynically (and happily) regard it as a phenomenon of your own creation, as evidence of your capacity for manipulating the media.

Nobody better exemplified this take on celebrity than radio controversialist and TV historian David Starkey. As he told me almost immediately after he'd sat down in the studio, he was quite happy with his self-description as an "all-purpose media tart". It wasn't in any way a piece of self-deprecation, a way of apologising as an eminent historian for his readiness to pop up on chat shows and espouse controversial opinions. It was rather "an advertisement".

And while such self-promotion might be inappropriate in the academic world of history, within the media it was a necessary trait. He had a reference to hand. "Remember Doctor Johnson making the wonderful distinction between the two activities of writing and talking. Writing is to tell the truth, talking is to win. And we're in a win world just now."

I told David that I'd recently been reading a very fine lecture of his on Henry VIII in which he'd referred to the king as a man who "strove consciously for fame". Did he acknowledge that degree of self-conscious planning in his own progress through the worlds of radio and TV?

He initially assured me that was not the case by telling me that he'd been selected for his first TV appearance because someone had described him to a TV producer as "the least boring historian at Cambridge". But when I pressed him on the "rude persona" he'd developed on BBC Radio 4's ethical chat show *The Moral Maze*, he readily agreed that he'd been thoroughly conscious of playing a part. He had, for the purposes of the programme, "dramatised" and "exaggerated" aspects of himself. But there was also an element of accident involved. On the famous occasion when he had come perilously close to "outing" a well-known archbishop on the programme, he went home thinking that he'd destroyed everything.

"And it was exactly 12 hours later that the telephone rang offering me the Talk Radio job with what was in those days, for me, unexampled riches."

David has never been shy about money. He remembered how he'd reacted when he'd been under attack for his latest outburst: the moment when *Daily Mail* published a picture of him with the banner headline "Is This the Rudest Man in Britain?" This, he told me, was immediately followed by phone calls from "real friends and especially false friends ringing, saying, 'Oh, David, we're so sorry. How can you live with this?'" And that's when he coined the triumphant response: "Well, don't worry darling, it's worth at least a hundred thousand pounds a year . . . and that proved to be a severe underestimate."

There was something familiar about this vulgarly exuberant reference to money-making which for a moment recalled a conversation I'd once had with Robert Kilroy-Silk. I'd known Robert when he was a Labour MP with a commitment to reforming the prison system, a commitment he'd completely abandoned in order to host his own confessional TV show, *Kilroy.* When I wondered in a Radio 4 interview if he had any doubts about giving up the politics of principle for the superficiality of show business, he told me immediately about the grandeur of his house and his swimming pool and his foreign villa with a degree of fervour that could only have delighted Doctor Freud.

But Starkey was different. His readiness to talk about money didn't strike me, as it had in the case of Kilroy, as a transparent way of rationalising his readiness to take the media shilling, it was more a romantic assertion of the physical pleasure to be derived from spending money on beautiful objects. He drives a Daimler, owns three houses, enjoys sporting a Rolex watch and expensive jewellery. I pointed out the rather flamboyant ring he was wearing.

"It's a very beautiful ring," he said proudly. "It's probably

Sheridan. It's – it's a 1780 whatever it is . . . in a rather lovely Art Nouveau setting. I bought it – I can remember the moment, the day, the shop. I bought it after I had made my first successful TV programme."

And, he went on to explain, "I just enjoy things. I enjoy the pleasures of mind. I enjoy the pleasures of the body. I love the feel of nice sheets, the taste of a good glass of wine. The taste and textures and smells of food . . ." And when I suggested that this extravagance and love of luxury seemed somewhat incongruous in such a serious academic, he was quick to disabuse me. "Much too much of academic life is a desiccation," he said. "It's a rejection. And I think it's one of the reasons that academics are so often such very bad judges and make such hideous mistakes. They don't and won't embrace a full humanity."

This argument adds some philosophical weight to Starkey's readiness to embrace the trappings of fame. Not only can he take pleasure from the fact that he controlled his own destiny, that he made himself in his own image in the notoriously cynical world of show business, but he can cite the aesthetics of money-making as a way of suggesting that it provides him with a better insight into the nature of the world than is vouchsafed to the academics who once constituted his reference group.

Tom Baker and Stephen Fry and David Starkey illustrate three rather different ways of handling celebrity. What they have in common, though, is that each had to cultivate a strategy from scratch. They were not brought up to expect fame.

Singer and songwriter Lily Allen had considerably more opportunity to learn how to cope with celebrity. She is the daughter of actor, stand-up comedian and man-about-the-Groucho-Club Keith Allen and film producer Alison Owen. And although she has claimed that her career was initially inhibited by her father's anarchic reputation, her huge success owes not a little to her obviously well-learned capacity for sophisticated

Lily Allen: "I know that I am Lily Allen. But I also know that she's not me."

self-marketing.

As soon as we began to talk, she readily admitted that it was irksome to be constantly recognised, to be constantly spotted wherever she goes, "whether it's the supermarket or whether it's, you know, going to the pub or a club in town or in the back of a cab." But what maddens her, she told me, is that the people who merely recognise her think that by so doing they actually know her. "The reality is that they don't know me. They don't know me at all. What they do know about me is something they're read in a newspaper which is something that someone has written about me."

And does that mean, I asked her, that she has an idea that there is someone called Lily Allen who is separate from her? "No, I mean I know that I am Lily Allen," she said. "But I also am quite realistic in the sense that I know that she's not me. If I believed all that stuff that I read about myself I would hate myself and I don't. So, you know, I have the ability to read and just go – oh, God, they're writing about that other person that doesn't exist."

Lily Allen was anxious to insist that she found her fame a little ridiculous. She comes down to earth, she told me, when she's with her boyfriend. "We sit at home watching *EastEnders* or *Coronation Street* and one of my songs will come on in the café or in the pub and I'll giggle. I just feel like, look, I really am a pop star. I'm on *Coronation Street*. And he just tuts and just goes, oh, it's ridiculous and, you know, we get on with our evening and that's it. You know, that's my attitude to it."

This dual-personality take on celebrity – the Lily Allen on stage is not the same Lily Allen as the one who sits at home watching *Coronation Street* on TV with her boyfriend – does seem an adroit way of handling celebrity, a way of separating the trappings of show business from the reality of life. But it makes rather less sense when we turn to Lily Allen's own songs. These aren't abstract musings on the nature of love and its affinity with the moon in June but deeply personal reflections on aspects of her own life. In her song 'He Wasn't There', for example, she vividly describes her ambiguous relationship with her own father and his fame:

> He wasn't there when I needed him
> No, he was never around
> His reputation was preceding him
> And he was out of town

It is difficult to see how any young person could respond to such lyrics unless they regarded them as autobiographical, as being somehow part and parcel of the singer's persona. Lily Allen may think that the "Lily Allen" who appears on the stage can be separated from the real Lily Allen. Her career depends upon the fact that her fans do not acknowledge any such dissociation.

In this respect celebrities at least can count themselves lucky. So eager are their fans to retain a consistent image of them that they can choose to overlook even quite gross contradictions. Fans of Frank Bough on BBC's *Breakfast Time* might have had to abandon their image of him as comfortable uncle in a homely pullover after the revelations about his cocaine-fuelled visits to a brothel. But nobody is likely to be disturbed by the knowledge that Lily Allen's most recent album, *Sheezus*, is heavily dependent upon her slagging off the very social media she so successfully exploited during her rise to fame, any more than Hugh Grant's dalliance with a Hollywood prostitute has put an end to his celebrity status as a good-hearted, bumbling romantic hero.

Lily Allen's use of dissociation as a way of handling her celebrity, her insistence that there was a Lily Allen who could be up on stage and another Lily Allen sitting on the sofa remarking on the peculiarity of that phenomenon, recurred in an almost pathological form in the shape of Uri Geller, a man I described in my introductory remarks as "either the world's most famous psychic or a charlatan". It was this very tension that intrigued me and that I wanted to explore in the interview. But after only a few moments' conversation he started to refer to himself in the third person: "The fame around Uri Geller that started with the trivial spoon bending came to a peak from which I could transform myself into the realms of pure motivational lectures."

And what did he personally do with the audience in these motivational lectures? "I remind them of what made Uri Geller famous. I do the spoons."

This was by no means an occasional usage. Throughout the rest of interview I was told about what "Uri Geller" did and what "Uri Geller" thought. It was as though the man sitting opposite me was relating the story of a person with an existence of their own, someone who only came into existence when the lights were switched on, the cameras focused. At times I even detected a certain weariness about the existence of this other being, as though it were a creation that had been willingly adopted at first as a career necessity – Uri Geller, the man with mystical powers – but had then developed a life of its own that was not always sustainable. He told me, for example, about the time, relatively early in his career, when he'd appeared on the Johnny Carson show in the States and had not been able to make a spoon bend in a manner that satisfied Carson, who was himself an amateur magician and "didn't believe in anything psychic". How did he cope with this failure?

"For 22 minutes I was sitting there sweating. And the only thought that kind of turned in my head: 'Uri Geller, you're finished. You might as well go back to the hotel, pack up and go back to Israel.'"

After the interview it occurred to me that this sense of having a public persona other than oneself had close parallels with early Hollywood stardom. James Cagney and Jean Harlow and Humphrey Bogart might have been distinctive individuals in their own right but at that time Hollywood's control over its stars meant their real life was never allowed to intrude upon their screen image. The very last thing the studios wanted was any touch of biographical reality or authenticity that interfered with that precious image. The stars weren't ordinary. That was their point. They didn't even partake of the ordinary. They had always been special. They had been born special.

This story could not, of course, be maintained when TV and the internet and other digital technologies made the previously protected stars into publicly available personalities. Once this happened they (or their agents) were required to produce a biographical story that managed to assert their authenticity, their ordinariness, without too profoundly disrupting their "specialness". Kirk Douglas on *Michael Parkinson* had to show us the Kirk Douglas we knew from the films but he also had to show us how, as Kirk Douglas, he responded to his own fame and reputation. He had to do something that was never required of the early stars. He had to tell us what it was like to be Kirk Douglas. This meant that in common with all contemporary celebrities he had to develop a distinctive take on his celebrity.

Part Two
For Art's Sake: Craft and Technique

Chapter Three

Making Music

Cleo Laine – Andre Previn – Nigel Kennedy – Harry Belafonte –
Joanna MacGregor

In my teenage years learning how to dance was not an optional skill. It was regarded by most young women as an essential proof of one's capacity to become a potential partner. Only those young men who had assiduously attended dancing classes and achieved bronze, silver, or even gold qualifications in the waltz, foxtrot and quickstep were deemed worthy of such modest erotic rewards as an open-mouthed kiss or a few moment of the furtive fondling the magazines called "heavy petting".

It was solely the prospect of these dubious treats that ensured my attendance every Saturday night at the Tower Ballroom, New Brighton, where I clumsily foxtrotted and quickstepped around the floor with my sweetheart Sheila Rogers to the strict tempo rhythms of Bill Gregson and his Broadcasting Orchestra. (Anyone tempted to display any distinctiveness in their dancing style, some modest assertion of their individuality, was effectively constrained by a notice attached to the right-hand pillar at the front of the hall which unequivocally declared, "No Jitterbugging.")

They were dreary times: times when there seemed a dreadful consonance between the strictness of the music's tempo, the formality of the dance steps and the rigidity of the moral code that governed my banal relationship with Sheila. It was, as my good friend Dave remarked a few years later as he recalled his own frustrated days of courtship, not unlike living inside a Playtex rubber girdle.

But then one night at The Tower everything changed. A notice outside the ballroom regretted the absence of Bill Gregson and his orchestra (no doubt they were busy fulfilling their much advertised broadcasting duties) and announced that their place would be taken by the Johnny Dankworth Band. I'd never heard of Johnny Dankworth but sensed that we might be in for a rather different sort of musical evening when the musicians strolled casually onto stage rather than striding regimentally to their allotted places.

But the difference really kicked in when they began to play. There was still a discernible rhythm but, rather than a rhythm that oppressively locked you into the next dance step, it was a beat that made you want to bend and break that step, to cut loose, to improvise.

Sheila did her best to cope but became increasingly agitated as her familiar one-and-two-and-three-together failed to mesh as they did so perfectly when Bill Gregson set the beat. Would I mind if she sat out the next dance?

I seized my chance. All I wanted to do was to get as close as possible to those wonderful musicians. Being near the front wasn't quite good enough. With a little effort I managed to scramble up on to the darkened side of the stage itself and squatted there with my legs dangling from the edge.

It was then that Johnny Dankworth introduced his singer. The band had been exciting enough but the entrance of Cleo Laine was quite overwhelming. She seemed to belong to a different species of womanhood from the plump, diffident Sheila Rogers. She was dark, exotic, proud, seductive. And she could sing like no one I'd ever heard before, could make her voice dip and soar and even echo the phrases made by the bandleader's alto saxophone. Her second or third song was the up-tempo "Perdido" and during the instrumental solos Cleo wandered over to my darkened side of the stage and sat down quite deliberately by my side. "Do you like the music?" she said in my ear. "Very very much," I whispered back, praying that, out there in the darkness of the hall, Sheila was watching her sad clumping dancing partner being touched by stardom.

Since that time I've seen and loved Cleo Laine and her artistry on any number of occasions but never again so close up and personal. When we met for the interview she listened carefully as I gushed through my story of our first meeting, then pulled the face that she must have pulled a thousand times when reminded by fans of a particularly memorable concert.

"New Brighton," she said slowly as though mentally checking off the thousands of gigs she's played during the 50-odd years she spent singing with John, years in she'd not only made a name as an actor but had also become the only female performer to ever receive Grammy nominations in three categories of music: jazz, popular and classical.

"New Brighton?" she asked again. "It really doesn't matter," I said. "Hardly anyone's ever heard of New Brighton anyway. It's over the river from Liverpool. In the old days it used to be a sort of resort. There was an advertisement that said, 'Visit New Brighton and watch the world's ships go by.' Of course, that was when Liverpool was a major Atlantic port."

Why was I telling Cleo all this? Why was I yattering on?

It's sadly something that I find myself doing whenever I'm face to face with musicians I admire. They're usually so quiet, so modest, so laconic, that I feel the need to fill the conversational vacuum. There's almost no limit to my yattering. I once yattered on to Johnny Hodges, the great alto player, when I found myself in the next stall to him in the Gents at the Royal Albert Hall.

But I know that I also yatter because when I'm with musicians, particularly jazz musicians, I'm always an outsider. Not really one of them. I might just be able to attract Cleo's attention for a few moments but I always know that the attention she pays to me will never resemble the attention (and admiration) she regularly bestows upon the musicians who share the stage with her.

I wondered if Cleo had possibly felt some comparable degree

of awe when she first met Dankworth. He was, after all, even at that stage, a respected arranger and alto player, someone she'd only heard on the radio before going to audition for him.

"What he liked about me more than anything else was that I had a very good ear and sang in tune. And when I went for a note, I was always on that note."

"But he changed you? He was a sort of Svengali? Changed your name?"

"That's right. I'm a Clementina really."

"Changed your favourite tipple?"

"Yeah. My drink at the time was brown ale and they didn't think that was the thing for a girl band singer to drink so they got me onto gin and tonic. Aren't men snobs and snooty?"

"So he changed your name and your drink?"

"And told me how to dress."

But if John Dankworth had any notion that he'd thereby come to own Cleo, he was in for a shock. Only a few years after becoming the band singer, she told him that she'd decided to go solo.

"I didn't want to be a band singer all my life. I had a feeling that there was something out there that I could do as well."

"And John reacted by ringing you up and proposing marriage?"

"Yes. I said yes."

"You didn't ever think that it was no more than a ploy to keep you in the band?"

"Oh, yes. Of course. I made a joke of it. I told him he was going to get a very cheap singer and a very expensive wife."

Cleo did indeed return to the band as John's wife but she was by now not merely a band singer, someone who came on stage in a pretty dress and sang words in between the instrumentals. Now she increasingly moved in on his music. She developed a sort of scat singing, something she preferred to call "vocalese".

It was all John's fault apparently.

"He used to write long intros to tunes and I got fed up with sitting there waiting for my entry," she remembered. "So I used to learn the musical intros and sing them. So when I did 'I'm Gonna Sit Right Down and Write Myself A Letter' – that was me singing the musical intro that he had written. And that's how our little act developed."

But given her huge repertoire, not to mention the range of lyrics she would have to master for her various acting roles, I wondered how on earth she managed to remember all her material: not just the words of the songs but the vocalese introductions. "I have got an excellent memory for words and songs," she said. "The music never exits from my head. The, um, the lyrics occasionally do."

So what does she do if that happens? She sings in Hungarian.

"We were doing a gig at Hampton Court a little while ago," she recalled. "I'd been singing 'Creole Love Call' for umpteen years . . . And, um, I started – started the song 'cause it just starts. Doesn't start with words, it starts with vocalese, and not a word came into my head. Not one word. So I started singing what I call Hungarian."

Not, of course, that she speaks a word of Hungarian. "No, the Hungarians wouldn't know what I was singing about," she agreed cheerfully. "And, um, so I – I was on one side of the stage and I manoeuvred over to John, still doing this sort of making up words and singing my ooblie dooblies and things and I went over and I said to him, 'Will you help me out with this song?' And he said, 'Nope.'"

To her credit, though, she wasn't fazed. She carried on – because you have to carry on. It's part of being a performer. In the green room before we recorded the interview, she was asked how, at the age of over 80, she still managed to retain the strength and quality of that distinctive voice. It was, she said, because she treated it with respect. She wasn't interested in belting out the songs as loudly as possible. That was just showing off, and could play havoc with your vocal cords. She treated the voice as her instrument, learned how to control it without forcing. It's a matter, she explained, of professionalism.

It wasn't only husband John who was concerned with keeping Cleo up to scratch. Her own children, Jackie and Alec, now both accomplished jazz musicians in their own right, would come to her concerts and prepare little graphs which recorded how well she'd done. "They used to give me marks out of ten. Jackie would say, 'Oh dear. You didn't get that high note at the end of the song,' or 'You were a bit out of tune there, Mum.'"

And she was forced to display another kind of professionalism, and an iron discipline, in the most telling of circumstances. On the day that John died, back in February 2010, she was due to perform at a concert at the family home in Wavendon. She nevertheless decided to go on with the show. "It was a hell of a decision – but there were 450 people there that had paid to see the show," she explained. "They didn't even know what they were going to see. They'd paid to come and see a show and they didn't know who was there. They didn't know that Maureen Lipman was going to be there, or Paul O'Grady or Victoria Wood."

The day before, she and her children had visited John in hospital, and he'd said he was determined to come to the concert. But he didn't make it. And despite her own feelings, she said, she did what he would have done. Which was – to go on with the show.

"I'm quite sure of that," she said. "Quite sure he would not have cancelled. So I got all the artists and musicians into the green room and I said that John had passed away and I would like very much to – to carry on with the concert. Maureen said, 'How are you going to do it, Cleo?' And I said, 'Well, I'll just have to do it.'" After all, "It was his memorial – a concert for him, 'cause he would have been there. I didn't even think twice about it."

Cleo was happy enough to talk about she and John related on stage, how he made her laugh, but her real enthusiasm was always reserved for his "brilliant brilliant music", for what they had achieved together musically on record and on stage. But hadn't she as a working-class girl from Southall also been somewhat impressed by the knowledge that they'd been adopted by so many famous fans, by the likes of Princess Margaret, for goodness' sake?

Not at all. "I never considered myself a working-class girl. I just considered myself a singer. If you've got a job then you're working. Margaret had a job too. She had to shake hands and smile all the time. I never ever envied any of them. I didn't want to be in that circle."

In my New Brighton days, I had little idea of what counted as jazz. There was so little jazz to be heard on the radio or in dance halls that when a new jazz record came out, perhaps a single from Humphrey Lyttleton or Chris Barber, we'd arrange an evening when we could play it over and over to each each other, mimicking the solos, beating time on the coal scuttle with a poker.

It's now customary to refer to that sort of jazz as "traditional", but at the time it was the only jazz around. All that changed for me and several of my friends in 1956, when Andre Previn sat down at the piano in a studio alongside two friends, drummer Shelly Manne and bassist Leroy Vinnegar, and recorded a jazz version of the songs from *My Fair Lady*.

That record was a long way back in the career of a man who'd gone on to become a concert pianist, a symphony conductor and a writer of acclaimed classical music. But when I met up with Andre Previn in New York, it was with jazz that I wanted to begin. Was there a first moment for him, something that perhaps resembled my lucky encounter with Cleo and Dankworth?

"A friend of mine from high school gave me an old 78 rpm

album of Art Tatum's and it was the first time I ever heard what can be done with 32 negligible bars in the way of stunning improvisation. And so I used to try and copy those records. I mean, note for note. Of all the insanely pointless things to do, because at the end of it what had I done? I'd copied it, of course, you know. But I started to veer away from it and have other favourites and then I began to have some kind of style of my own."

He went on to describe how his mastery of scoring informed the production of his acclaimed jazz version of *My Fair Lady*. "Well, none of us knew the whole score," he recalled. "So we had to send out to an all-night record shop, which was called Music City. And he came back with a record and we played one track at a time and I learned the tunes and then we played all night. And at the end of the night we had a record made." And that record sold over a million copies.

While Previn is unendingly versatile in his choices of musical forms, I wondered how he coped with having such a firm foot in both the classical and jazz words. Weren't the classicists among his friends a little snooty about jazz, a bit ignorant perhaps?

He nodded in agreement. "Well, yes, I know, for instance, that Anne-Sophie Mutter did not know much about it except Louis Armstrong." (He was referring to the renowned German classical violinist, once his wife, still a very close friend.) "I wanted to know where her cut-off point was," he explained. "And I finally put on a record by the Basie big band and she went bopping around the house, she adored it. So I thought, okay, all right, now I know. And – and I think of that old, old hoary old joke of Fats Waller's who said to the woman who had said, 'What does swinging mean?' And he said, 'If you got to ask, honey, don't mess with it.'"

But didn't he himself have any blank musical spots? I knew he could readily range across classical and jazz but what about the avant-garde, experimental, freeform music?

"Cage and Ligeti and all that? I like that very much."

Where there any exceptions?

"Well, when I hear a new piece, a really, really new piece in a concert hall, and I go out at the interval and a composer friend of mine says, 'Very interesting,' I always think, Oh, Christ. 'Very interesting' is not what I want to hear. Do you remember a composer called Terry Riley? Well, he wrote a piece called "In C". Which was a C major tonic in all its possible shapes and permutations. But that's all there was, for about 15 minutes. And I thought, Well, yes, and I walked out and there was Morton Gould [American composer, pianist and conductor], who was a very funny man. And I said, 'Martin, what was that?' And Martin said, 'It's terrific, I'm going home to write an arrangement in B flat.'"

I reminded Previn of another wonderful musical joke: his appearance in 1971 on *The Morecambe and Wise Show*, where he'd had to suffer a range of indignities, from being routinely described as "Mr Preview" to being told that he was incapable of conducting Grieg's Piano Concerto.

"I loved doing that. I thought they were such nice fellas. In London taxi drivers still holler at me in the street and call me 'Mr Preview'."

Did he in any way relish that kind of celebrity, the kind of public fame he'd also surely acquired through his marriages to such high-profile figures as Dory Previn, Mia Farrow and (his fifth marriage) Anne-Sophie Mutter?

In a way I already knew the answer to such a question. I'd seen Previn only recently playing and conducting at the Barbican Hall in London and been quite moved by his modesty on stage. His whole demeanour announced that it was not he that mattered but the music. Fame and celebrity had to know their place. Music was always the master. Becoming better at music was always the goal.

"Hindemith once said there's no such thing as too much technique. And that's a good thing to say. I know that when I'm conducting something complicated or writing something complicated or somebody says my part is horn in E flat but they've transposed it to G and I've got it written in F, at any time where I don't quite know where I'm supposed to be, then I know I want more technique. You can never have too much of that. I like knowing."

It is perhaps the prestige accorded to classical music that also ensures a degree of modesty amongst its performers. Classical orchestras are typically dressed in evening clothes whose conformity of colour and style reduces the possibility of distraction. And while soloists are increasingly permitted a degree of flamboyance in their dress and in their style of playing, anything that might be construed as "disrespectful" to the music or its composer can quickly become the object of noisy censure.

Nobody in the classical world has been so indicted for this form of *lèse-majesté*, for allowing themselves to become part of the celebrity game, as violinist Nigel Kennedy. I can still recall my own ambivalence towards him as I prepared for the interview. (A close friend was appalled that I was going to "give him any more publicity".)

I had no doubt, however, about his ability: for years I'd been delightedly playing a CD featuring his performance of Beethoven's Violin Concerto. But I wanted to ask if he really needed to speak in that voice, to don such wholly unconventional, even "disrespectful", clothes, in order to promote his distinctive image. Such crass self-promotion did seem rather better suited to a rock arena than a philharmonic hall. Wasn't he exploiting the cult of celebrity?

Perhaps he could take me back to the time when his onstage clothes had first gained attention. How much had he deliberately set out to shock?

"There was a big element of accident. I'd left my orthodox classical gear in New York in a cleaner's and I'd got back to London to play a straight classical concert with the Royal

Philharmonic. It was a Sunday and the only place open to buy replacement gear was Camden Market. And all there was there then was some black punky stuff."

And what had been the reaction to his appearance on stage in punk gear?

"I thought the orchestra was very pleased that I'd actually broken a few taboos. The conductor was a bit uptight because I was upstaging him. And after, I thought, 'Why should I ever get into uncomfortable clothes again? I'll stick with this type of stuff. Be comfortable. That's the main thing.'"

But wasn't there something a little disingenuous about this account? Surely it wasn't just about being comfortable, it was about using clothes and hairstyle and accent as promotional techniques?

"I'm not the Florence Nightingale of music. I didn't set out to play classical music to save it from predatory upper-middle-class people. I started playing because I wanted to share enjoyment."

I knew that that sense of enjoyment with music hadn't always been around. I reminded him of the days when he'd been sent off at the age of just seven to the Yehudi Menuhin School of Music in Surrey. Remember?

"Oh, yes. I was surrounded by muesli and yoga and music. Yehudi had very strong altruistic and philosophical ideas but there was nothing like a family background or atmosphere. In my first three years there I think of myself as having gone into hibernation."

It was the visit of French jazz violinist Stéphane Grappelli to the college that woke him from that slumber.

"He said, 'Does anyone want to play?' And I had my violin under the seat and was ready with all the Fats Waller stuff: 'Ain't Misbehavin'', 'Honeysuckle Rose'. And he was so impressed that someone from another generation could play that stuff."

Playing with Stéphane was clearly a musical delight for Nigel. But what he also learned from him was that music-making could be far less austere and puritan that he'd been led to believe by the College. For "whereas the muesli and the yoga were okay for Yehudi, for him it was spliff and a whisky. And there's nothing like a bit of ganja to get the barriers down."

Nigel talks a great deal about bringing down barriers. He's always on the lookout to disturb his own and other people's preconceptions. Anything that breaks up the ordered surfaces. When John Drummond, the controller of Radio 3, famously attacked him for his "grotesque, self-invented accent", he was happy to explain.

"There were people I admired – jazz musicians who represented another world outside the poncy classical world – and I possibly latched on to their accents." And then there was that punk haircut.

"Yeah. One time I got it cut really short and everyone in this suburban place when I lived started walking on the other side of the street to me. And I thought, 'That's interesting.'"

"It had the desired effect?"

"Yeah. The barriers went down a bit. And also with my colleagues on stage. They [think], 'We'd better get on with the music because we're not going to be following some pre-ordained route. We've got to listen.'"

Harry Belafonte: "I always use the power of my platform to give something to other artists."

When I knew I was going to have a chance to talk to musicians, to understand the nature of their commitment to their craft, and perhaps learn how such commitment protected them from some of the excesses of the celebrity culture, I did not for a moment think of adding Harry Belafonte to my list of hopefuls.

I'd certainly known about the singer for many years but in common, I suspect, with many others in the UK I'd primarily associated him with a couple of sentimental ballads and a rendering of "The Banana Boat Song", which in truth I'd always found somewhat less appealing than the pastiche version by Stan Freberg ("Too loud, man.")

But then, almost by accident, I read his extraordinary autobiography, *My Song*, and realised that my knowledge of the man's life and work was probably so inadequate because Belafonte's 60 years of commitment to radical political causes had meant that he was afforded only grudging recognition in the patriotic American music and entertainment scene. In common with his hero Paul Robeson, he'd learned that the cost of his radicalism was the disparagement or even denial of his talent. But it did not appear to have made him the least bitter. For what he had in common with Cleo Laine and Andre Previn and Nigel Kennedy was not only a life devoted to music-making but a deep belief that such involvement had prevented him from becoming distracted by such ephemeral matters as celebrity and fame.

Even before we sat down together in the New York studio, I showed him a 1950s black and white photograph of a bass player and an alto saxophonist.

"Aha," he said instantly. "Charlie Parker and Tommy Potter."

"You knew them both when they were that age?"

"Oh, yes."

It all began, he told me, in the '50s, in a jazz club in New York City called the Royal Roost. "At that time the club had a huge significance globally on the music scene in America. It was the introduction of modern jazz, it was the introduction of a style called bebop, and if you wanted to know what this new music was doing and what the new innovators were creating, this was the Mecca. And everybody came to listen to these great artists of the day – Coltrane, Thelonious Monk, Charlie Parker, Lester Young, Dizzie Gillespie. I mean every great artist that was in this modern world of modern jazz came to this scene."

At that time, Belafonte would never have been able to afford seats at a place like that. He was a drama student, studying in a theatre nearby. "And every night at the end of a production a lot of us students would retire to the Royal Roost and for a 25-cent bottle of beer we could stand at the bar in the back among what we called 'the scholarship crowd'. A lot of us young students stood there and listened to this great music night after night."

And who was in the group? "Walter Matthau, Rod Steiger, Bea Arthur, Marlon Brando and Tony Curtis, who back then was called Bernie Schwarz. All these students went night after night down to this club. And through these many weeks and months we became familiar with a lot of the musicians. They asked us what did. We said we studied theatre. 'What do you study in theatre?' Lester Young said. And I remember saying to him, 'Well, I study acting.' And he looked at me for a moment and said, 'How do you do that?' I found the question rather challenging because from that day till now I've never been able to answer anybody who says, 'How do you study acting?'

"Anyway this led to us inviting these artists to come see what we did. Now, you have to understand that not only were these jazz musicians creating a new style and a new approach to this music, but also here were a group of actors working with a German director from the world of the Max Reinhardt theatre in Germany. And these young actors were learning a new form of acting, a Stanislavski method approach. So we were the theatrical counterpoint to this group of musicians who were this musical counterpoint to what we were doing as actors. And when these guys came to see us, one of the plays they saw was a play in which I happened to have been cast as a character and in that play I was required to sing a couple of songs.

"And they heard me. And one day at the end of this drama I was slowly running out of resources. I no longer had a government subsidy to go to school, I couldn't get any work as a black actor. What was I doing studying to be in the theatre when there was nothing for black actors to ever do? But one night down at the club I told them with some trepidation about my conflict of not being able to continue. And Lester said, 'Why don't you sing some songs?'

"I thought he was jesting. And he said, 'No, I'm very serious.' I said, 'I'm not a singer. You've got all the great singers in the world here, Ella Fitzgerald and people.' I could not see myself in that space. But he said, 'Talk to Monty.' Now Monty Kaye was the impresario of the club, a very young guy, about 23 years old, very smart. And he had booked for this club and brought all these great artists together. And he listened to this plea put in by these guys. And he said, 'Okay, let's give him a shot.' I said, 'I don't have a repertoire.' And Monty said, 'I'll take care of this.' And he went out and picked a pianist to help me build my repertoire, my first ever repertoire. And the guy they picked was by the name of Al Haig, one of the great jazz pianists of the period."

So he worked with Al Haig for several weeks putting a tiny repertoire together. It was just meant to fill in the 15-minute interval while they changed audiences, while the new customers were being seated. Belafonte imagined he'd only be on stage with the piano player – but it turned out to be rather more dramatic than that.

"And when I came out for my grand moment, just Al Haig and myself, I walked up and Al played the intro and, just as I was about to start up, in walked Tommy Potter, the bass player. Well, I enjoyed the idea that he was going to sit in but no sooner had he got his bass up when in came the drummer, a man by the name of Max Roach. And then the last of the Mohicans was Charlie

Parker. He came and hooked his horn up and all of a sudden my first night ever singing to the world at large as a professional had a backup band: Charlie Parker, Al Haig, Tommy Potter and Max Roach!"

And that "anointing", as he put it, the generosity those great musicians showed him as a young artist, established for him a code of behaviour that he followed for the rest of his life. "I always use the power of my platform to give something to other artists. I say, 'Use this platform and play to the audiences that I play to.'"

Despite this memorable debut, though, Harry Belafonte didn't feel completely at home with jazz music. Something, he felt, was missing "Listening to Ella Fitzgerald, Louis Armstrong and Nat King Cole and the great practitioners of that art, I really realised that I was quite minimal in that circle and, because I couldn't find my voice, I couldn't find the way in which I wanted to express myself."

So he changed career entirely, even for a while doing a stint as a short-order cook in Greenwich Village. But he never stopped going to listen to music. "I wound up at the Village Vanguard and then I met two men that changed my life, one by the name of Woody Guthrie, great American folk artist, and the other man by the name of Leadbelly, another great American."

He heard both of them at the Village Vanguard. "I went night after night listening to these artists, inspired by them. I went out and began to listen more intensely to the folk music of America, went down to the Library of Congress and stayed there going through hours and hours of folk . . . almost the entire Alan Lomax collection and the recordings of others. And I discovered in that world the first inspiration towards using the power of the song to communicate social thought and social ideas. And I really worked very hard at learning the form and finding my own style with it.

"I was very much influenced by Paul Robeson, the great artist of that time, a man of enormous social and political courage. He meant a lot to a lot of people in the world and I admired him greatly not only for his art but his social thinking. And out of that I began to shape my own life in the world of folk songs. And I put my repertoire together and in that repertoire were songs I recalled from my childhood, songs from the Caribbean, growing up in the mountains of Jamaica, and all the lilting beautiful melodies that the people sang, and I made those part of my repertoire."

Belafonte's account of his musical journey, the manner in which his life was measured out in different musical forms, has many parallels with the other musicians I interviewed. Unlike other celebrities, they have an external yardstick against which they can measure their talent and their development. Actors and other stage and TV performers often seem uncertain about the nature of their talent, uncertain how they might measure themselves against others in the profession. Instead of talking about their career as a step-by-step progress, they're far more likely to characterise it as having been dependent upon little more than luck or good fortune, having been in the right place at the right time. Musicians can appear as easy-going and disorganised and genially anarchic as any other performers, but the best among them always seem to possess a vein of seriousness, a "commitment to a muse", which is never for sale on the altar of entertainment, never influenced by luck or circumstance. Their technique always places them in an acknowledged hierarchy.

Nobody better captured this distinctive commitment than the concert pianist, conductor and composer Joanna MacGregor.

I'd wanted to interview Joanna primarily because of her musical eclecticism. It's not at all unusual to find primarily classical musicians like Nigel Kennedy and Andre Previn playing jazz and playing it supremely well. But even in such cases there's always a slight sense that they are taking a holiday from classical music, being slightly indulgent, playing away. But Joanna MacGregor never seems to have turned to jazz as an alternative form of music: it always seems to be close at hand and therefore oddly unremarked in nearly everything she does. Indeed, even while she was undergoing her extensive classical piano training at the Royal Academy of Music, she was kicking against the pigeonholing effect of classical music education.

"I've always been very inspired by jazz musicians because those structures weren't there. Jazz musicians could continue to be fully rounded. They were very entrepreneurial about doing their own recordings, releasing those recordings on their own labels, writing their own music. Doing all those things that a baroque musician would have done."

It's appropriate then that when Joanna does play music that would normally be filed in the box called "jazz", she rarely draws attention to its category. On the CD *Play* that I listened to over and over again before I went to meet her, a jazz stomp sits happily alongside music by Bach and John Cage and György Ligeti.

What Joanna seemed to relish most in her favoured music and musicians was the unexpected, the unpredictable. She heard it for the first time at the age of 14. At a stage of her life when she was "sweeping up and down the piano" in pursuit of her goal to be a concert pianist, she was given an unusual present.

"My dad bought me an LP of Thelonious Monk for my 14th birthday. I thought it sounded really odd. All you could hear was this person going clang, clang, clang. And I just kept on listening until I thought, 'This is absolutely fantastic.'"

It seemed extraordinary that a 14-year-old should have been so persistent with something so apparently dissonant. What was it she came to love about this music?

"It's fantastic from a professional pianist's point of view because Monk plays as if he can't play. He sits at the piano and slams it, and makes weird and dissonant noises. And suddenly it's very fast, very awkward, rather brilliant. It's the antithesis of the brilliant virtuoso playing that had come before. It's a sort of anti-playing, which I've always found really beguiling and attractive. It makes you think about the purpose of playing, about why one does play and why one would choose one note as opposed to another note."

But was she also attracted to Monk and the way he played because of what she had learned about his eccentric character? She had, I knew, written a very successful radio play about Erik Satie, the early twentieth-century composer and pianist who was hardly known for his conventionality.

"I like Erik Satie in the way I like John Cage and I like Charles Ives. I like people who lead rather devoted singular lives but are fairly light about it. That's a great skill."

"Light?"

"Yes, what they're all doing is deadly serious but they behave as though it's only a way of living. It's something I aspire to: that sense that one can be quite light, quite questing, but not heavy. Not laborious."

Chapter Four

Making Art

Tracey Emin – Damien Hirst –Grayson Perry – Ralph Steadman

Tom Baker once told me that when he was young he only had one ambition in life: he wanted to become a martyr. It was an easy enough ambition for me to understand. Even if martyrs were, almost by definition, required to endure horrific deaths, I knew from my Catholic upbringing that they were not only the most worthy objects of praise and adoration, but beings with an automatic guarantee of eternal life in heaven.

I had a rather more earthbound ambition. I wanted to be an artist. For although there were no theological grounds for believing that artists had any special claim on a happy afterlife, there was plenty of evidence that they were, like martyrs, persons deemed suitable for praise and adoration during their mortal life. One had only to switch on Sunday-evening TV to see the extent of this appreciation. Artists who graced the late-night arts programmes were rarely if ever quizzed about the nature of their craft or forced to answer questions about their actual merit. They had, by some magical mechanism, been transformed from artists into Artists, and once that transformation had been effected it was no more appropriate to ask about their craft or their worthiness than it was to ask a martyr about the appropriateness of their eternal home in heaven.

This meant that when I was deciding upon the contemporary artists I wished to interview for *In Confidence*, I chose those whose standing, even in the idolatrous world of art, was still the subject of debate and controversy. Tracey Emin and Damien Hirst were obvious candidates.

But I was also anxious to question the nature of what came to be called 'art' by talking to two people whose extraordinary skills had not been enough to secure them admission to the pantheon: the graphic artist Ralph Steadman and the potter Grayson Perry.

Tracey Emin: "I invented my language. You have to crack the code."

Tracey Emin hardly needs to fret any more about her public status: she's enjoyed a major exhibition at the Southbank Centre and another at Turner Contemporary in her home town of Margate. But we're not far into the interview before she starts to talk about those who fail to pay her proper respect.

"There are critics what'll always criticise me. Always. I can name them right now. But why slag me off? I'm not doing anything. I'm not stealing their territory. I don't understand why they take the piss out of how I talk or the way I look."

Her insecurity in the face of some of these attacks is evident from the manner of her defence. Look, she says, I've got some proper qualifications.

"I'm not one-dimensional. I'm an artist. I work hard. I spent seven years at university. I've been a senior lecturer at The Royal College of Art. I've got a doctorate of letters."

Perhaps, I suggest, some of the criticism she attracts is prompted by concerns about the explicit biographical content of her work, its depictions of her tragedies, her abortions, her sexual promiscuity, her fractured relationships.

But these aspects of her art, she insisted, were not depictions of her life but transformations: that legendary *My Bed*, which was first exhibited at the Tate Gallery in 1999, was her way of transforming something ugly, something debauched, into beauty. She'd woken up with an appalling hangover, was terribly dehydrated. "And then I went back into the bedroom and I looked and I thought, 'Oh, God, it's disgusting, ugh.' Everything was so dirty, so filthy, so horrible. And then I looked again and then the next thing I saw was my bed, and I thought, 'That's not disgusting, that's not dirty, this bed has kept me alive. This bed has kept me up, kept me buoyant.' And I looked at it and as I looked at it, I imagined it in pristine white, beautiful – like heaven. A pristine white beautiful space. I thought, that's really beautiful. And then I took the bed and I put it into a show in Japan."

As Tracey Emin quite reasonably claims, plenty of other artists have taken everyday aspects of their own existence as subjects for their art. Nobody seems exercised in any way by the knowledge that Van Gogh spent time painting his favourite chair. It is readily accepted that by this means a singular personal object was transformed into something more universal. Tracey claims no more.

"My subject isn't me," she insisted. "My subject starts with me and then it goes to the rest of the world."

But surely, I asked, didn't her use of such personal subject matter as her own abortions in her art represent a far greater degree of biographical revelation than Van Gogh's portrayal of his favourite chair?

She allowed that this might be so but argued that her greater self-revelation was in tune with the individualism of our time.

Twenty years ago, for example, journalists would rarely have used the first person when they were writing, but now, said Tracey, this degree of self-referencing was quite normal. There was now, in her words, "a palate" for her art. Her language had been learned and become acceptable. That was the key to success. The absolute key.

"I invented my language. There are so many brilliant artists out there whose work is appreciated and adored. But they'll never be seminal because they didn't crack the code. It's like being a scientist or an inventor. You have to crack the code."

Even though I've come to appreciate and even admire much of Tracey Emin's work, this doesn't blind me to the manner in which her present degree of fame is at least partly the result of her being promoted by the art market, a market whose practitioners are as sensitive and skilled at creating and promoting celebrities as any branch of show business.

And, of course, as we have already seen, contemporary celebrities of whatever order are now all required to have biographical back stories that in diverse ways authenticate their public claim to be special kinds of people. In this sense Tracey is a gift to publicists. She not only has a vivid back story. She also makes it the starting point for her art. She truly is a child of the times.

Celebrities in the world of art do, however, face a problem about authenticity that troubles celebrities in other spheres to a far lesser degree: money. Rich rock stars who chat about the need for a working-class revolution, or celebrity hosts on charity shows who display delight at having raised a sum for *Children in Need* that hardly matches their own annual salary, are suitable cases for little more than some genial satire. But although we may not wish our contemporary artists to starve in garrets as a guarantee of their vocation, we still cling to the idea that artists should somehow preserve a distance between the integrity of their artistic practice and the machinations of the market. There's not too much concern about paintings by dead artists raising millions of dollars at an art auction. After all, such artists may well have paid their poverty dues during their lifetime. But for a living artist to enjoy massive mercenary acclaim invariably raises suspicions about the true value of their work – particularly when that work seems explicitly designed to shock or arouse controversy and is heavily patronised by a leading figure from the cynical, soiled world of advertising.

Damien Hirst is fully alive to all such criticisms of his wealth and his patronage by Charles Saatchi. Indeed, as I discovered during our interview, he is, in many ways, not only happy to confront such attacks head-on, but also to admit that he exploits them for his own benefit.

He told me readily how thrilling he found it to be recognised not just by the art world but by businessmen. He positively liked the idea of rich wives getting money from their husbands to buy art. But, even better, "I quite like the fact that the husbands were suddenly going: 'Who is that Damien Hirst?'"

But behind this brash recognition of the manner in which his celebrity helps to sell his works lies an almost obsessive concern to place himself firmly within standard artistic traditions. "I am a traditional artist," he explains, an artist who sits firmly in a continuum of artists from Michelangelo to Hirst's early mentor at Goldsmiths College of Arts, Michael Craig-Martin.

Not that he ever expected to secure any place at all on the artistic continuum. Back in the early days in his home town of Leeds he was only too aware of his shortcomings.

"I never thought I'd ever be a famous artist. Early on at school I wanted to be the best drawer in the class. We were drawing dinosaurs and there was this one kid who was the best drawer and I used to think, 'Oh, I wish I could be like him.'"

And it was in his home town, in the aquarium that used to sit under Leeds City Art Gallery, that Hirst came across some of the sights that were to have such a significant influence upon his later work.

"There were all these strange crazy things in the aquarium. I remember axolotls (a type of salamander closely related to the tiger salamander) in jars and tanks. The kind of wonder you get in The Natural History Museum."

Hirst talks frequently about the power of an object to arouse "wonder", about the moment when you find yourself confronted by "something that makes you go wow in your mind. Objects have this incredible power to seduce or confront viewers . . . think of a tree. You walk past it every day and you become unaware of it. But it falls down and it's this enormous thing. You can't stop looking at it. So all you've got to do with an object is just move it."

It was, I suggested to him, a perfect account of what might have lain behind his famous shark-in-formaldehyde installation, *The Physical Impossibility of Death in the Mind of Someone Living*, even if it didn't explain the wholly original way in which he'd chosen to "move" this particular object around in order to nail the viewer's attention.

He bridled at the word "original".

"If you look at any artist, their work comes from the past, from other artists' work. If you look at Van Gogh's *Sunflowers*, you're also looking at [the 18th-century French artist Jean-Simeon] Chardin's sunflowers. When I grew up in Leeds I was definitely thinking, 'I've got to be original.' But then afterwards you think it's impossible to be original. Once you look up at advertising billboards and at movies and at the barrage of influences from everywhere, there is no way you can be original. There's no way that originality is important. Visual language is made of every-thing since the beginning of time.".

But wouldn't he want to accord some sort of originality to his more startlingly inventive constructions? What about *A Thousand Years*, the glass case containing an actual life cycle with maggots hatching and turning into flies, which then feed on a bloody severed cow's head, while other hatched flies meet their violent end in an insect-o-cutor. That was hardly derivative, was it?

"Oh, yes. You can say the fly killer, the blue of the fly killer is like a Bruce Nauman, the boxes are like Dan Graham, the cow's head's like a Bacon, and the flies themselves are like a Naum Gabo in *Points in Space.*"

Quite a collection of artists. But not one of them, however honoured, had ever made so much money out of their art in such a short space of time as Hirst. What that something that really made him especially proud? Or made him feel over-valued? Or just extraordinarily lucky?

"I think money's a fantastic tool to get people to take you seriously. Money is like a key to the world. It's something you have to respect, something you have to come to terms with, something you can't avoid . . . I've always thought it a real shame you [the artist] don't get it till you're dead. I remember [American art dealer and gallery owner] Larry Gagosian said to me, 'Van Gogh never sold a painting in his life.' As though that's some sort of comment on me being at the other end of the spectrum. But when I was a kid I didn't have any money . . . So the thing I loved after the auction [the sale of *For the Love of God*, a human skull recreated in platinum and diamonds] was walking down Bond Street and getting recognised by businessmen."

Only in the last few minutes of the interview did Damien Hirst back away slightly from his customary almost jaunty readiness to be judged at least in part by his enormous financial success.

Was it true, I asked, that Francis Bacon had been to an exhibition of his in the Saatchi Gallery and afterwards told someone that he'd spent half an hour looking at the fly installation?

"Yeah, that's right."

"And weren't you hugely impressed that someone you admired so much, someone whose work you've loved ever since you saw it at an early age in Leeds Art Gallery, stood for half an hour in front of one of your works?"

"I didn't believe it when they told me."

And then for the first time in the interview, Damien Hirst became self-deprecating, almost hesitant.

"I think," he said, "that was the only piece of my work that he liked."

But even this seemed to strike him as insufficiently modest, insufficiently respectful of a true hero.

"Probably wouldn't like any of the others," he added reflectively.

It was a very different kind of modesty that first attracted me to the ceramicist Grayson Perry. I'd invited him onto a radio programme to discuss *The Craftsman*, a book by sociologist Richard Sennett that lamented the contemporary decline in craftsmanship and sought to emphasise the rewards that came from using tools, acquiring skills and thinking about materials.

Grayson had seemed an obvious choice because not only had he repeatedly insisted on referring to himself as a craftsman but also because his chosen metier, pottery, was conventionally regarded as a matter of craft rather than a form of art.

During the course of the discussion, I asked Grayson if his decision to call himself a craftsman had been a difficult one to take. After all, it did, in the context of radical modern art, seem almost like a deliberate declaration of unfashionability. What room was there for elaborately decorated plates and vases and pots in a world containing such truly modern sensations as Tracey Emin's *My Bed* and Damien Hirst's formaldehyde shark?

Grayson was only too happy to concede the point. "To tell the truth," he said, "it was probably easier for me to come out as a transvestite than as a craftsman."

In our interview I was anxious to know how this insistence upon the craft nature of his work influenced his view of other contemporary artists. It was, he explained, all about the work ethic.

"You've got to put in the man hours. That show of mine at The British Museum [*Tomb of the Unknown Craftsman, 2011*] is probably three, three and a half years' work if I added it all up. Many man hours."

But that amount of work was often overlooked by those who relished a particular image of the modern artist.

"The *coup de théâtre*, the dramatic gesture, has become . . . associated with the romantic idea of the artist. You know, if you see an advert that has got an artist in it, they've always got a bit of paint on their face and they're always chucking paint about in this romantic passionate gesture whereas my work is a war of attrition! You know, it's plod, plod, dib, dib, for hours and hours and hours. And I think that young people, because they can do something on *YouTube* very quickly with digital culture, they think that's what art is like. But you've got to put in the hours."

But didn't he feel this romantic stereotype was also perpetuated by those contemporary artists who sought to disturb and shock with their conceptions and installations. Those who regarded themselves as radical or cutting-edge might surely lose some of their impact, their street credibility, if they described the weeks and months that went into the construction of their dramatic images.

"I think contemporary art now is ordinary. The idea that art is this radical cutting-edge challenging thing – this is a trope that needs re-examining. People accept art now. When Antony Gormley's empty plinth stood in Trafalgar Square, there was a thing about it on *The Archers*. Linda Snell was enthusiastic about it! If Linda Snell is enthusiastic about conceptual art, then it's not cutting-edge."

It's simply not shocking any more?

"I think the art world kids itself that it's this dangerous teenager . . . People now accept contemporary art in all its difficulty. There is a different set of values now."

No one who's seen a Grayson Perry exhibition would wish to suggest that his subject matter was tame or conventional. Indeed there's a special charge about seeing such startlingly explicit sexual imagery on the side of a piece of pottery that might otherwise have almost domestic connotations.

Grayson is also fully alert to the manner in which his work breaks down existing categorial distinctions. He instances Duchamp's famous *Fountain*, the standard porcelain urinal laid flat on its back that the artist submitted for an exhibition in 1917.

"That was something from ordinary life which [Duchamp] brought to the gallery and said, 'This is art.' A very clear kind of boundary was crossed there. Now, a pot has kind of one foot in an art gallery already. That's where the discomfort lies. It's almost a class thing. Oh, a pot! 'We don't want those lower-middles in a gallery.'"

So what made his pottery troubling to the experts and the punters was the sense, as it had been with Duchamp's *Fountain*, that it was somehow out of place. His works were not only reminiscent of "mere" craft but they also suggested an almost suburban origin that seemed totally at odds with the modern idea of art as radical and shocking.

His pots, he told me, also stood apart from other contemporary art by virtue of their inability to prompt the type of intellectualism that has become associated with conceptual art.

"People are much better educated nowadays, and so, of course, there are always going to be people who regard intellectual difficulty as the prime quality of art. That idea has taken too much precedence over the last hundred years . . . critics and talkers love conceptual art . . . because you can waffle on about this and that, whereas to actually pin down why a certain painting is more beautiful than another painting, you have to have visual sensitivity."

Grayson may suspect people who write and talk about art, but his own pieces frequently have a literary content. Satirical messages about consumerism, the mass media and prudery are frequently scrawled on the side of his pots and vases.

"Yes, I just react to the moment. The satirists and commentators I admire the most and aspire to be like are the people that spot the very tufts of the ears of the new sacred cow coming over the horizon. And they're brilliant people because they can shoot at it before it's on the turn."

Even though I was happy enough to talk to Grayson Perry about his pots and his messages, I knew the moment would come when I had to ask about the manner in which his transvestism had, whether he engineered it or not, acted as a publicity device, a way of ensuring that he stood out from the crowd, an aspect of his persona that helped constitute him not just as an artist but as a celebrity artist.

He was immediately anxious to explode the idea that there was anything cultivated or manufactured about his cross-dressing.

"You don't decide to become a transvestite when you're a sophisticated adult. The roots of that are laid down when you're a small child and they're hard-wired by the time you've hit puberty . . . It's because it's a childish thing that you're kind of trapped in your desire to do it, compelled to do it throughout your entire adulthood even if you go on to be Lord Chief Justice."

But even if, as he claimed, his transvestism was a matter of compulsion rather than choice, he could surely still accept that it enhanced, or at least amplified, his public status?

"I don't even think about it from one month to the next. I'm not embarrassed about any of it . . . The media can be very lazy about reassessing people. So often when you come into the spotlight you're defined for your whole career by that first step .

. . We all develop and change but I'm still that potter that did those shocking pots and dresses as a woman. That's my thing. If you're gonna have a brand, it's not bad. It's done me a lot of good."

But Grayson Perry is not alone in practising in an area that refuses to fit neatly into traditional or avant-garde ideas about what is art. That same confusion applies to the work of the illustrator and cartoonist Ralph Steadman.

I first came to appreciate his capacity for conjuring up nightmarishly comic visions through my reading of Hunter Thompson's drug-fuelled, anarchic *Fear and Loathing in Las Vegas*, published in 1972.

I was so taken with the power of these drawings, their extraordinary combination of spidery lines and exploding blobs of ink, that I had the temerity to ask, via a mutual acquaintance, if he'd draw a caricature of me for a weekly column I was about to begin in *Times Higher Education*. He agreed, and asked for a photograph to help him with the likeness.

When the caricature arrived, my partner of the time objected. It was, she insisted, not a good likeness. Even as a caricature. I must take it back to Mr Steadman and ask politely for a revised version. Unwillingly, I did as I was told. "My partner thinks it doesn't quite do me justice," I explained, hovering on his doorstep. "I wondered if you'd mind – erm – having another go?"

Without a word Ralph marched me and my picture upstairs to the back room of his Fulham house, where he promptly pinned up my gaunt, elongated image on the easel and proceeded to add two circling bats above my hair, and insert a large metallic bolt through the lower half of my neck. "There," he said. "That should protect you from ever writing anything bland in your column."

Thirty years later I'm still writing that weekly column and there have indeed been plenty of occasions when I've looked at what I've written and been forced to recognise that in terms of shock value it singularly fails to live up to the anarchic Steadman image.

But I also knew from following his career that Steadman himself was always concerned about the continuing potency of his work, about whether he was living up to his often expressed wish to do something to change the world. Why, I asked at the beginning of our interview, did he no longer produce the savage political cartoons that had once enlivened the pages of *Private Eye* and the *New Statesman*?

"I actually have not the slightest interest in politicians any more . . . They don't seem to have any guiding sense of clarity or honesty . . . I feel we're not democratically ruled any more. We're ruled by regulation."

I wasn't too surprised by this sentiment. I knew from past conversations with Ralph that he had been greatly influenced in his early years by such anarchist thinkers as Max Stirner. Someone with that philosophical background was eventually going to find that there was a limit to the satisfaction they could obtain from lampooning here-today-and-gone-tomorrow politicians. But what was the alternative?

Ralph explained that he'd turned instead to people of ideas, to people like Sigmund Freud and Leonardo da Vinci. In his books on these figures he'd broken new ground. He'd been able to explore their ideas in writing as well as in drawing. That suited him very well.

"I was never sure whether I was supposed to be a writer or an artist – or, for that matter, an aircraft engineer, which is what I was when I started life."

Had these shifts in direction done anything to diminish his huge energy? I reminded him of what he'd said to me nearly a decade earlier when, in an interview for the magazine *New Humanist*, I'd had the audacity to ask if he'd become less anarchic, rather more gentle? At that time he'd brusquely dismissed any such idea.

"Oh, I'll never get any smoother," he'd told me. "I'll get edgier and edgier. I'm in a hurry. Picasso is a sort of role model for me. At the end of his life he was doing three or four paintings a day or he thought he wasn't living. Right into his 80s he was producing painting after painting, entire series of etchings. Hundreds of etchings. Old self-portraits, haggish women, beautiful voluptuous figures. And cavaliers. People said, 'Where are the cavaliers coming from?' He explained that he'd been watching Errol Flynn on TV. That's great. Really fucking great. Anything that's going on. Absorb it. Reconstitute it. Keep fucking going."

So, now, a decade later, was that energy still there? Had anything changed? Anything that might affect his vigour?

Yes, something had changed. His great friend and collaborator Hunter Thompson had died. People who knew them well together still say that Steadman was the wilder of the two, or rather that Steadman only felt he had permission to be as fully anarchic as he wished to be when he was alongside Hunter. Ralph told me how he heard the news.

"It was Joe Petro from Kentucky who rang me up and said, 'Take your phone off the hook. Hunter's just shot himself. He took a Magnum 44 and put it in his mouth.'"

And his death had made a difference?

"Well, it was an event. A whole period of time passed from when I met him in 1970 to the time he shot himself in February 2005. Yes, something did die with him. I no longer use the style I'd have used if I worked for the *New Statesman*. Now, it will be something idiosyncratic, slightly odd . . . I do gentler drawings now. Gentler drawings of butterflies and cats and dogs. And I say, 'What am I doing this for? This is a crazy way to carry on.'"

Butterflies and cats and dogs?

"Yes, butterflies and cats and dogs and insects. Yes, insects. Little tiny bugs . . . I suddenly thought, 'Why don't I do bugs? Because I'll be seeing them anyway in the not too distant future.'"

Chapter Five

Making Laughter

David Schwimmer – Michael Frayn – Howard Jacobson

Analysts of TV celebrities are fond of using the term "parasocial" to characterise the relationship that exists between the viewer and the figure on the screen. It's a way of capturing the sense that we somehow know and feel a special kind of involvement with our favourite newsreader or our favourite sitcom or soap opera character. Unlike the magnified figures on the cinema screen, they seem accessible, almost domestic, almost part of the familial furniture.

The term implies that when I watch an episode of *Cheers* or *Frasier* I can simultaneously know that I'm watching carefully crafted, beautifully produced, lovingly scripted performances from professional actors and yet also somehow believe in the biographical reality of the characters they assume. "Frasier's behaving very badly tonight," or "It doesn't look as though Sam's going to get anywhere with Diane using that line," I'll say to my partner. On one occasion when I heard myself expressing such sentiments, I had a brief moment of shame. What was happening to my critical judgement? I was watching a programme artfully prepared for my delectation by a commercial TV network. How could I possibly be implicated in any meaningful way with how "Frasier" was getting on with his brother "Niles", or whether "Sam"'s banal chat-up lines would ever be effective with the self-consciously arty "Diane"? My partner was reassuring. "It's only natural," she said. "They're all our friends."

It was because I'd spent so many happy hours in such parasocial contact that I frequently found myself wondering what it would be like to come into face-to-face contact with one or another of my sitcom heroes. Even though it would be Kelsey Grammer or Ted Danson or Shelley Long who would be sitting in the chair opposite me, rather than Frasier or Sam or Diane, their long-standing and hugely successful performances in those parts must surely mean that something of their fictional characters resonated with their own personality. Ted just had to be a bit like Sam for Sam to seem so very real.

Charles Guerin © Sky

David Schwimmer: "I didn't want to be locked into playing one part."

My chance to test this hypothesis depended on a lucky break. One of my partner's friends had a daughter who'd been employed for a time as a waitress in a relatively high-class London restaurant. One evening she had served David Schwimmer, who plays Ross Geller in the massively successful American sitcom *Friends*. A friendship had developed as a result of that chance meeting. By the time I met him they were married, with a small daughter.

I'd exploited the contact for all I was worth and was finally rewarded with the promise of a New York interview. But even as I relished the news I began to realise that I would hardly endear myself to David in such an interview if I concentrated too much on the character he played in *Friends*. It would hardly to do ask him questions about why he had so many failed relationships, or why he was so often clumsy and awkward, or how he felt about being bossed about by his stage sister Monica. I had to remember I would be meeting David the man, not Ross the character.

But the TV crew in our New York studio looked likely to be far less circumspect. Several were so excited at the prospect of meeting Schwimmer that I had to issue a public warning. "Please," I entreated in the green room, "When you see him face-to-face don't make any reference to *Friends*. Treat him as a very distinguished and very interesting actor. Not as Ross."

As the interview began, I strained to keep the conversation reasonably objective. I talked about the craft of comedy rather than about Schwimmer's specific part in *Friends*: the rather geekish plaintive character who is always trying to do the right thing and making a botch of it. Was there some form of comedy that he particularly relished?

"I love physical comedy," he told me. "When we first started *Friends* they gave me a few things to do and they saw that I could not only do it, but I could repeat it. I think that's the trick. That's what technique is. That's what training is. Being able to do it not just once but to do it over and over again. And as we were filming in front of a live audience what became really fun is that repetition, seeing how many different ways I could trip or open a door and walk into something.

"I think the impulse came from my love of making my family laugh. That was the greatest pleasure. There was nothing greater than the sound of my parents laughing because of something I'd created or something I'd done. I would hurl myself around the furniture and bounce everywhere. I've broken countless bones, I really have, growing up."

His very first appreciative audience he told me, was his sister Eleanor, who was only a year older than him.

"I would try to recruit her, to make her laugh. But I also loved terrifying my sister. That was a great pleasure, just hiding in cupboards knowing when she was coming home from school and planting myself in certain areas and jumping out and scaring her."

It sounded sadistic.

"No, it was just fun to scare the hell out of her. It was funny. And back then I also watched a lot of comedians: Buster Keaton, Charlie Chaplin, the Marx Brothers, Abbott and Costello. And I have to say that Inspector Clouzot was a huge influence for me. And a lot of cartoons. Cartoons are a big influence on physical comedy. Especially *Road Runner* and *Wile E. Coyote* [an animated series on American television]."

All these expressions of interest in comedy seemed a perfect explanation of why Schwimmer had found the part of Ross in *Friends* so appealing. But he was anxious to tell me that before he was cast in the part he'd thought of abandoning TV series for good. His experience in a short-lived CBS sitcom called *Monty* had not attracted him to the genre. And in any case, "I wanted to play a lot of characters in my career. I didn't want to be locked into playing one thing."

It wasn't as though he didn't have alternative acting opportunities. He'd established with fellow drama students his own theatre group in Chicago, The Looking Glass Theatre Company. And this is where he felt his true vocation lay. What could be better than working collectively, in a tight-bound group with like-minded people, to produce good serious drama: the kind of acting that he'd always wanted as his own after seeing Ian McKellen playing Richard the Third?

He saw the look on my face. "Yes, I studied and trained and worked really hard to develop that versatility only to be really known for playing one guy. Ironic."

So why did he go back on his resolution? Why become Ross? Why end up playing just one character for nearly a decade?

It seems that he was in Chicago with his theatre company working on a new play when his agent called.

"And she said, 'I know you told me no more TV shows but I really need you to read this one show.' And then she said the key word to me. She said, 'It's an ensemble of six people. So you're just one of six.' I said, 'Ahh! I'm not doing it. But send it to me anyway.' And I read it. And, of course, it was hysterical and I immediately identified with Ross and where he was emotionally."

So David Schwimmer took the part and even now, a decade after the last edition of *Friends*, he is still widely seen as Ross. People simply assume that he must be prudish, meticulous and awkward. I reminded him of the occasion when a fight broke out in a bar where he was drinking, a fight between two women, one of whom had confronted him and loudly berated him for the way in which Ross had treated his pet monkey.

"You know, I think there was a time when that sort of thing really irked me. But I guess not any more. Life's too short. I decided years ago that it's out of my control."

Schwimmer came to realise that his portrayal of Ross, however beautifully timed and exquisitely executed, would be consistently under-estimated by all those legions of fans who thought that he was doing little more than being himself.

This misidentification seems to afflict comic actors and comedians rather more than their serious or even tragic colleagues. Although it is well recognised that the character of "Hancock" owed a great deal to the writing skill of Galton and Simpson, we are still inclined to believe that the "Hancock' we know from radio and television is either a direct representation of the person called Hancock or is based on extensive obser-vation of that persona. If anything, this view perversely gains more rather than less credibility when we learn about the tragic outcome of Tony Hancock's attempts to find a comic identity other than that assembled for him by Galton and Simpson.

Not that comedy needs to rest upon elaborate or even credible characterisation. When I knew that I was going to be talking to Michael Frayn, I was determined to ask him about the comic genre in which he excels and in which none of the participants needs to be burdened with biographical baggage: the farce.

Frayn, of course, has written explicitly serious plays such as *Copenhagen* and *Democracy*, as well as an ambitious and provocative philosophical treatise, *The Human Touch*. But he will not even countenance the argument that he was taking a holiday from such seriousness when he wrote his farcical play *Noises Off* and his more recent farcical novel *Skios*. Farce, he insists, is a deeply serious business.

"When I first started writing farce, interviewers would always say, 'Why do you write farce? Why don't you write about life as it really is?' I couldn't imagine what their own lives were like. Because endless farce *is* my life."

And, he told me, he was not alone in this.

"We all have some fear inside ourselves that we won't be able to go on with the show, that the conversation will dry up, that we won't be able to say anything at all. And people do have breakdowns, they do sit down in the corner of the room and feel unable to go out and face the world. And I think to see that happening to somebody else in ridiculous circumstances, to see other people unable to go on with the show, is a real release for one's own fear."

But how did he respond to those who mistrusted or disliked farce because it didn't allow for character identification? Hundred of thousands of young men no doubt recognised themselves in Ross Geller but what was anyone to make of the ciphers who inhabited farce?

I reminded Michael that no less a playwright than George Bernard Shaw had disliked farce intensely for the simple reason that it offered no opportunity for the audience to identify with any of the characters on stage. To laugh without such sympathy was "a ruinous abuse of a noble function".

Michael looked less than impressed.

"Well, I see his point. But consider Henri Bergson, one of the great theorists of humour. In his book *Laughter* he proposes that comedy arises when human beings behave like machines. And that applies to farce. People are behaving like machines. You do get bits where the door is flung open and simply hits someone on the behind and they fall on their face or whatever, and that's quite funny. But it is also funny to see someone who you know is in a desperate situation and can't think how to get out of it. And you also know that whatever they do it's going to be wrong. Make matters worse."

I knew for myself how well this worked on stage, particularly when the dramatist and the director could come up with one of those wonderfully orchestrated series of farcical events with accident piled upon accident, calamity upon calamity. If it was as well done as it had been in the two productions I'd seen of *Noises Off*, it could reduce sizeable sections of the audience to something approaching hysteria. But hadn't Frayn now gone and written a novel called *Skios* that he talks about as a farce? How could a farce work on the page?

"Well, in novels I've written before there's been quite a lot of farce. But yes, *Skios* is nothing but farce. It may not work at all because in the theatre with a lot of people laughing you can't help but respond to that laughter. My hearing is now bad but I've been in the theatre and although I couldn't hear what was going on on stage, because other people laughed, I laughed with them."

Could he name any other novel in the long history of literature that might be called a farce?

He thought for a moment. "No, I don't know one. But I always like to be a way-maker for everybody else. I suppose we shall have to see whether it works or not."

I thought about the novel and its capacity for arousing real laughter, noisy laughter, when I knew I was going to be interviewing Howard Jacobson. Although he hadn't been the first novelist to make me laugh out loud at words printed on a page – that "first" was shared between Joseph Heller in *Catch 22* and Kingsley Amis in *Lucky Jim* – I could readily remember having to pause for a breath several times during my reading of Jacobson's early campus novel *Coming from Behind*.

After that I became a sort of Jacobson groupie. Indeed, I was so amused and entertained by some of his television reviews in the *Sunday Correspondent* that I sat down one day and wrote him a fan letter. "Thank you so much for being so very observant about popular television and so very, very funny."

I enjoyed his comic take on life so much that before I went to Australia for the first time I sat down and read *In the Land of Oz*, in which he describes his own travels around the country. My companion on the trip wondered at several stages of our journey if I was capable of seeing anything for myself, some event or circumstance or sight that hadn't already been filtered through Jacobson's perversely comic imagination.

But, of course, my chief and ever unfolding delight was always the novels: *No More Mr. Nice Guy*, *The Mighty Waltzer*, *Kalooki Nights*, *Zoo Time* and the 2010 winner of the Man Booker Prize, *The Finkler Question*.

I was, when reading these, always waiting for the joke, for the comic turn of phrase, the farcical circumstance, the banana skin. Although the reviews of these and other books often told me that Jacobson's novels had higher philosophical concerns – the nature of English Jewishness, the meaning of lust, metropolitan anti-Semitism, the decline of the novel – I was like some late-night drunk watching an old sitcom. To hell with the metaphysical meaning, to hell with the turns of the plot and the acute characterisation. Where's the next joke?

Even though this did make me a somewhat crass reader of Jacobson's work, it also meant that I subsequently became especially intrigued by his own attempts to beat away the label of comic novelist. Why, I wondered, as I read his protestations, was he so very anxious to resist such an appellation? It wasn't as though the literary world was heaving with comic writers. Shouldn't he celebrate what, in the view of myself and many critics, made him so refreshing, so distinctive?

But, as he quickly told me when I raised this question in our interview, he hadn't always taken this line on his work.

"I never had any choice as a writer. I thought I had a choice. I thought I could be a solemn tragic novelist. That, and that only. And when I tried to write as a young lad, that's where I tried to go and got nowhere. Absolutely nowhere."

As these early pretensions faded, as his hopes of becoming a Henry James for our times receded, Jacobson found himself consciously lowering his sights, making a virtue out of literary necessity, settling for something other than great literary fame.

"It seemed to me like an acceptance of an inferior career for myself. All right, this is going to be the best I can do, so I'll do it. And the 'it' was comedy."

But this proved to be only a grudging acceptance. For, as his reputation grew, as critics found more than good jokes in his work, Jacobson rebelled against his own designation. Yes, he admitted, I do write comedy, I do make good jokes, but that is not because I belong within that peculiar bookshop category "comic novelist", it is because, plain and simple, I am a novelist.

Jokes and humour, he began to argue, are not elements that are added to a novel like a sprinkling of nuts on a cake; they are an endemic feature of all language. Humour is not a supplement, it is always there waiting to be found: an ever-present in language.

"I have to begin by looking for the joke that's in the language. The sculptor looks for the sculpture in the stone. I look in the language. I don't think it's just a matter of me having to invent: it's there. You start writing and immediately you've put ten words on the page, there's a joke. By a joke, I mean something bigger than 'Take my wife.' There's something in there, in language, there's a play in language, something you want to be doing with the words, and then a little bit later with the situation, and then a little bit later with the characters, that's screaming, screaming for comedy. And if I can't find it, I've failed. So I become obsessive about finding the comedy."

This insistence upon humour being an intrinsic feature of language allows Jacobson to shrug off the comic-novelist label, not because of its demeaning resonances but because of its essential meaninglessness. "Show me a novel that's not comic," he asserted, "and I'll show you a novel that's not doing its job."

But did this mean that he'd wish to put down those authors who failed to find the comic in language? How about George Eliot? Wasn't she often described as lacking in humour?

"You've touched the problem case for me," Jacobson admitted. "Because I do think *Middlemarch* is the most wonderful novel. It's one of the few exceptions I'd make to my normal argument, which is that if a novel isn't funny I don't want to read it. I do want to read *Middlemarch* and it's not funny. But there are very, very few other novels I would say that about. If it's not making me laugh in some deep way, not necessarily laugh out loud, but if it's not twisting the thing around and making me feel uncomfortable, if it's not saying, 'I'm going to make you think something completely different,' and if the language isn't robust enough for me to hear the actual voice of the writer, then I'm out of there."

I wondered how much of this belief in the omnipresence of humour informed his life outside literature. He might be unable to hear the voice of the writer in any novel that failed to play with language in a humorous way, but this did this mean that he might in real life be inclined to devalue those who appeared to lack a sense of humour? It did.

"I always suppose that if anybody hates me it's because they have no sense of humour. It's something you can't cross. I think in a friendship with somebody, if they're not funny, if they don't make you laugh or if you don't make them laugh, there is no friendship. There is no love. There's no love between a man and a woman when there is no laughter. Laughter, for me, has always had a huge erotic component. And in friendship, what are you doing with somebody with whom you don't laugh?"

Neither, as Jacobson once argued in a radio interview, were there any limits to the occasions upon which laughter might be thought appropriate.

"If you really believe in comedy, that comedy is an indispensable activity along with intelligence, then you just can't drop it. It can't just not be there when people start dying: if it's going to be any use at all it's got to be there when there is the greatest sadness."

And as Jacobson's reference to comedy in the face of death implies, humour is not a gentle social lubricant, a way of announcing togetherness or solidarity. Quite the contrary. It is often confrontational, vicious, shocking. It is "always looking for someone to punch, always looking for something to kick."

In this, he is happy to go along with Bergson's view of humour as a social corrective, as a means of restraining certain kinds of behaviour because of the "fear it inspires". In Jacobson's words, "In every humorous situation there must be a winner and a loser: if not, this renders the situation humourless."

It is this emphasis upon the fear at the heart of comedy that has led Jacobson into tricky territory. There may always need to be a winner and a loser in every humorous situation, but what about those situations in which the loser in the joke is already an object of contempt or discrimination? Are we, for example, expected to relish the jokes that Bernard Manning makes about Pakistanis because this is simply the way humour works? Or should we object to such jokes because they reinforce a view of the world that we would otherwise reject?

Although I suspect it has lost him some liberal friends, Jacobson remains consistent. He not only defends Bernard Manning but is said to have attended his shows and even gladly offered himself up as the butt of his anti-Jewish gags. A joke is a joke is a joke, he insists. It is not a statement of either a belief or an opinion.

"Once one accepts that a joke is in a structured dialogue with itself, that it cannot by its nature be an expression of opinion, you have conceded the un-alikeness to racist discourse, which by its nature is impermeable and cannot abide a contradiction."

This seemed to suggest that those who failed to appreciate a joke, who confused it with some other form of discourse, were lacking in insight – in intelligence.

"Of course it's intelligence. Freud said the Jewish over-valuation of intelligence was at the heart of all this. Humour is an act of the intelligence. Getting the joke is an act of intelligence. Making the joke is an act of intelligence."

But if humour, like intelligence, is intrinsic to a person's nature, how might we explain those who were formerly funny, but now seem to have surrendered to seriousness?

"I know exactly what you're talking about and I look at it with the same kind of concern that one looks, at my age, at things like Alzheimer's. I see it as a matter of intense personal necessity to go on being funny. I don't want to write books that aren't funny. I want to write books that are all sorts of things but they must always be funny. So I got very disappointed by the later Philip Roth. I swear by Philip Roth, but Philip Roth is not funny any more."

Hadn't I seen Roth quoted as saying that there simply wasn't anything to be funny about any more?

"He must have the right to say that. And Woody Allen must have the right to say, 'After what's happened to me, what's so funny?' But I just don't really buy it. You're not funny because there's something funny. The whole point of the Jewish joke is that the Jewish experience isn't funny . . . Philip Roth should be more than ever making jokes . . . I don't know what's waiting for me. I could leave this studio and be struck down with something terrible and life suddenly wouldn't strike me as funny any more. But I hope to God, yes, I hope to God I can go on being funny."

Chapter Six

Making Stories

Andrea Levy – E. L. Doctorow – Michael Frayn

"Hello," I said. "Is that Malcolm Bradbury?" "It is," said that voice at the other end of the line. "I'm so sorry to bother you," I said. "But my name is Laurie Taylor and I write a weekly column for a magazine called *Times Higher Education.* It's a sort of satirical column about what's happening in our universities. Anyway, they've decided to publish a collection of these columns and I was wondering if you might be prepared to write an intro- duction." I paused and waited. "You did say, 'Laurie Taylor', didn't you?" said Malcolm. "Yes," I said. Why did he need to ask again? Hadn't I been clear enough? "We've never met, have we?" said Malcolm.

Although this exchange took place over 20 years ago, it is still fresh in my mind because of the strange example it provided of the manner in which fiction can rub up against reality.

For, as I was to learn later, Malcolm Bradbury had been considerably disconcerted by my call because, although we had indeed never met, he had been repeatedly told by readers of his famous campus novel *The History Man* that the character of Howard Kirk, the energetic and spirited young academic sociol- ogist who appears centrally in the book, was based on me.

In an essay published some time after our conversation, Bradbury expanded upon the sensations aroused by my call.

"It is not a natural thing for an author to be telephoned out of the blue by one of his own characters," he explained. "It is a crisis we share, Professor Taylor. I do not know you; you do not know I. I have not met you, and by the same token you have not met me. Yet I have invented you, or on the other hand you have been invented by having been invented by me . . . we are bound together in some strange and unexpected symbiosis as origin and simulacrum, writer and written. Yet just who has done what to whom it would take Jacques Derrida to explain, and I am told he is too busy."

When I knew that I would be interviewing several celebrated novelists for the Sky Arts series I resolved to spend some time playing with similar paradoxes, talking to each one of them about the peculiar relations and correspondences that existed between the real world and their artfully assembled fictions.

I knew as soon as I saw the TV dramatisation of Andrea Levy's fourth novel *Small Island* in 2009 that she had a very distinctive account of the reality-fiction issue. For, as the dramatisation revealed and the book itself confirmed, Levy was telling an intensely personal story not simply about the arrival of Jamaican immigrants to this country back in 1948 but also about the vicissitudes that befell her own family and, in particular, her mother.

Small Island contains some immensely moving scenes: the moment when the well-mannered Hortense discovers that her hopes of continuing her Jamaican teaching career in England are dashed by the discovery that she lacks the appropriate English teaching certificate: the scene in the hospital where the father is dying of lung cancer. How closely did these stories parallel the experiences in her own family? Hortense must surely be based on her own mother.

She insisted that it was not that simple: the characters were fictional. Properly fictional. They resembled but were not the same as their real-life counterparts. "That's what you do in fiction," she explained. "Otherwise all I'd be doing would be writing biography, non-fiction biography." And she had techniques for avoiding that possibility. "I take stories from everywhere and mix them up and play around with them and give them back to you in some other way."

But wasn't it the reader's sense that she was writing about her own mother that gave a special intensity to the fiction? "Surely Hortense's story is your mother's story as she must have told it to you?"

No, insisted Andrea, that really wasn't the case. In fact, her mother positively disliked talking about the past. It was, as far as she was concerned, almost a closed book. And better kept that way.

"It was only as I was getting older that I myself began to get a real interest. Only then that I realised this was an incredible story! A story that hadn't been told well, or told that often as a story, a story that everybody thinks they know already. I wanted to hear it from her. But it was still hard to get her to talk."

And the reason for that silence also spoke to the difference between reality and fiction. Her mother distrusted writers. Why? Because she didn't want her privacy invaded or placed on display. "She didn't want people knowing what she considered to be private family matters."

"She didn't want people knowing your business?"

"Yes," said Levy. "Knowing our business. Yes, absolutely."

I noticed that the word "story" occurred frequently in Levy's accounts of her craft. It was rather as though she thought of the real historical world as containing any number of untold stories and it was the job of the novelist to discover such stories and bring them to life. This quest to bring narrative to bear upon historical events, to give a voice to what was previously mute, is perhaps most evident in her award-winning later novel *Long Song*. Far from containing any element of autobiography, this was an historical novel that sought to create a different world, a world that was once horrifyingly real: the world of slavery.

Levy was prompted to write it, she told me, by the remark of a young woman at a conference she had attended. The woman had demanded to know how she, Andrea, could be so apparently proud of her heritage when her ancestors were slaves. "And I thought, 'I wonder if I could change her mind by telling her a story?' And I suppose that's what I want to do with all my fiction. I wonder if I can change people's minds by telling them a story they've never heard before."

But tackling the theme of slavery was not something she greatly relished, partly, she admitted, because the research was so upsetting. "To go into that period of time, to immerse yourself in it for six years, to come across the worst of human nature and see the way in which its repercussions are still with us today . . . it could, you know, put you off people!"

And another reason for her hesitancy in approaching the project was that she didn't think enough people would be interested. "It's a subject we don't really talk about in this country. We love to talk about slavery's abolition but the three hundred years before that gets left out a bit. And I wasn't sure that the people in this country were ready to listen to the story of slavery, the story of British slavery, and understand it."

And once she did start the novel, she quickly found the research couldn't be confined to libraries. She had to go to see for herself how much legacy of that time still remained. And she was surprised by what she found.

"There's so much left of slavery," she told me. "I went to a plantation because from my desk in Crouch End it was hard to imagine such a place. I needed to experience the expanse of it, and to hear and to smell it and to understand it. And so I went to a plantation in Jamaica, one where the great house of the owner was almost intact, where there were lots of water mills and a limekiln and you could really get a sense of the geography of the place. It helped me to understand how very industrial the sugar process was, and how slavery was part of that industrialisation."

But there was more. She told me that she also needed to see the fields of cane that had to be cut at harvest time, and see the cane being milled, in order to understand the nature of the work that had to be done not just by men but by women and children too. There were hardly any testimonies from the slaves themselves that could help her in this enterprise. But she discovered that she could bring to life some of their previously silent voices by reading through the pamphlets and memoirs that had been left behind by people like the planters' wives and the missionaries.

She was particularly taken by a book written by Mrs Carmichael, a planter's wife. "I suddenly discovered that I could see through what she was saying to the life beyond. She talks about her Negroes being so rude and lazy because they stood in this room and just looked at her. And then later she could hear them discussing her clothing from her head to her toe. I thought, 'Wow! I'm seeing something different. I'm seeing a life and an energy.' The white people were always writing about things like parties and they'd say, 'Oh, the Negroes came up and they stayed for two days making music.' What?"

It was from such writing that Andrea Levy began to see a different image from the one that she'd gained from reading about slavery in fiction, where she'd always encountered the slaves as little more than victims. "Suddenly I was glimpsing their real lives. For three hundred years these people had actually survived and thrived. And I wanted to celebrate that."

This wish to move away from victimhood, to provide the slaves with a voice of their own, a life away from the plantation owners, is perfectly realised by Levy's decision to hand the narration of the story over to July, a mulatto, the daughter of a Scottish overseer who'd raped her slave mother. July was born and brought up on a Jamaican slave plantation and has strong ideas about how to tell her own story, even though we learn from time to time that her memory is inaccurate, that she is a fallible narrator. It is a clever way for Levy to tell an important story while at the same time drawing our attention to the way in which storytelling develops an independence of its own, an independence that is always threatening to dishonour or pervert reality.

I relished the manner in which Levy simultaneously told stories while all the while using a fictive device to throw some doubt on their literal or emotional accuracy. But when I knew that I was to interview one of the greatest novelists of our time, E. L. Doctorow, I recognised that I would be faced by an almost completely original way of binding reality with fiction. For in his work Edgar Doctorow not only uses memories and characters from his own life, he also incorporates real historical figures. So *The Book of Daniel* was based on the story of Julius and Ethel Rosenberg, who were tried for treason for allegedly passing nuclear secrets to the Soviet Union and executed in 1953, while his most celebrated novel, *Ragtime*, teems with iconic historical characters: Henry Ford, Houdini, Emma Goldman, Sigmund Freud.

It was, as I soon learned when we sat down to talk in New York, an approach to fiction and reality that he saw as no more than part of a grand tradition. Historical fact was always bumping up against fiction.

"When I was a child and growing up I read Dumas, and Cardinal Richelieu was a character in *The Three Musketeers*. And in another piece Tolstoy takes Napoleon down, calling him a silly fat little fellow who can't ride a horse properly and whose shoulders quiver when he's upset. So I'd always seen the use of real people in fiction. But *Ragtime* had a kind of satirical edge to it; I thought of it as a mock historical chronicle. And it was published at a time when fiction was relatively quiet and timid and at the same time when the non-fiction writers, the new journalists, were employing fictive tropes to persuade the reader – and I got a little upset with that. And also the sociologists and anthropologists were doing fictive things, doing group portraits of various ethnic groups and so on. So I felt we novelists were being pushed aside. And I decided, 'Well, if they want facts I'll give them facts!'"

I could understand how he found his license for mixing fact

and fiction in existing literature, but surely he went much further than the other authors he'd cited? He agreed.

"Although I thought I was doing what writers had always done, at the same time I did have a sense of transgression. I find that, in any work I've done, as long as I have that sense of breaking rules or doing something I shouldn't be doing, the work will come out all right."

Doctorow uses real people in a rather different way in *Homer and Langley*, which is closely based on the notorious eccentric hoarders the Collyer brothers. These very real people are translated into mythical figures in the book, they are given an historic importance they never enjoyed in their real lifetimes, they become a way of reflecting on and even redefining history.

"What I like about that book *Homer and Langley* is the possibility that by collecting all this junk they became curators of the American civilisation. They didn't have to do that, they came from wealthy backgrounds, socially upper scale, but nevertheless decided to become recluses and eccentrics and I never thought of them as psychological cases. I treated them as a myth. They're still a great myth in New York City. When their establishment was gone and done and the police and sanitation department came in and unloaded stuff from the house, crowds collected outside that house and every newspaper was covering these people. So they were sort of an urban myth in my mind and I treated them as a myth. I changed the location of their house and I gave them another 20 years' life and put them opposite Central Park. I felt I could do with them as the Greek playwrights did with the house of Atreus, just do my own version of those two guys. And another thing that appealed to me was the idea of them being aggregators, sort of like Google. They were offering you a museum of your own history."

That mythologising of American history and culture permeates all of Doctorow's work. His first novel, *Welcome to Hard Times*, was a kind of homage to the genre of the western. It began, he said, as a parody of the form. "I realised perhaps I could do something with this disreputable genre that was worth doing. That's how that novel got to be written and I thought I did pretty well never having been west of Ohio. But then I got a letter from a woman in Texas. By her hand I could tell she was an elderly lady, it was a very fine shaky hand. And she said, 'Mr Doctorow, I was with you till Chapter Five when you have a cowboy eating the roasted haunch of prairie dog for his dinner and I knew at that point you'd never been west of Ohio because a prairie dog haunch wouldn't fill a teaspoon!'"

Undaunted, he told me, "I simply wrote back and said, 'Well, that's true of prairie dogs today, madam, but this book was set in the 1870s. They were much bigger than prairie dogs now.'"

While many of his books are set in the past, Edgar Doctorow rejects the label "historical novel" with much the same ferocity that Howard Jacobson seeks to dispatch the label "comic novelist".

"Any word that modulates the word novelist I would resist. And, of course, in a sense every novel is a historical novel. All novels take place in the past, the near past, the far past. It's a way of labelling things to contain them. It doesn't stand up under examination. How about the fact that Hemingway and Andre Malraux were both writing about the Spanish Civil war while it was going on and one of them published a book during the war and the other just after the war and that was 75 years ago and do we think of them as historical novels now? It doesn't make any sense. I think what happens is that the time the book was written falls away eventually and there's only the internal time of that novel."

Novelists, argued Doctorow, couldn't allow themselves to be constrained by conventional over-simplified ideas of how time worked.

"People have the illusion that time is something that flows from the past to the present and the future. The physicists have a very tough time with the idea of time; it's an enormous problem for them. The flow of time. There's a book called *Eternity to Here* [by the physicist Sean Carroll]. The author says it's fine if you talk about a river flowing from one place to another. That's okay. It's flowing from one location to another. But where does time flow from? It has no location, it just flows from itself. So we novelists can employ basic physics in defending what we do. Einstein discovered that time was the fourth dimension and you can extrapolate from that to a view of the universe as an enormous book where every event recorded is occurring simultaneously throughout the whole universe."

I told Doctorow that I could recognise many instances of this resistance to the flow of time in several of his novels. He didn't speak about historical events as though they were in any way consigned to the past. They were somehow ever-present. I wondered therefore whether one theme in his writings is a kind of resistance to the idea of history as progressive. Consider the Cold War, the subject of *The Book of Daniel*. People would like to think that was all over, but Doctorow doesn't want to allow that it is. It still has lessons for us. It still counts.

"Well, I suppose there's something of that but it would be rather dangerous for a writer to say, 'I'm going to give you a lesson.' I don't think that's the way my mind works. What I discovered earlier and I think fortunately was that I could use a chunk of time the way another writer used a sense of place. Why that occurred to me I don't know, perhaps because I'd lived in an urban environment with no sense of the slow passage of time you might get in another part of the country like the South or West. A piece of time, I realised, could be as much of a constructive principle for a novel as a sense of place. So Faulkner would have his deep South, and I would have the first decade of the twentieth century."

I pressed him further on this notion of the myth of progress. What I found in his books was a refusal to go along with the idea that civilisation was constantly improving. His books seemed to be saying that any long look at the past teaches us that we're merely deluded if we talk about the world as not only constantly changing but actually improving.

"Let's put it this way. I'm using a set of images to reiterate the insufficiency of the human race. And the images may change but the insufficiency in all its varieties is available to the reader. I see what you're getting at but I would tend to resist any implication that I feel morally superior and granted myself the enlightened position to instruct everyone."

But *The Book of Daniel*, the most explicitly political of the novels, does directly seem to attack the way in which the American Communist Party betrayed its purpose by becoming too inward-looking. It failed to recognise what was going on in Stalin's Russia at that time. And there is a lesson to be learned from this myopia.

"Well, of course a novel with any substance to it deals in ambiguity and different readers will take different things from it. People will often ask me to certify their opinion of this or that book and I will never do that. I can tell you how that book [*The Book of Daniel*] came to be written. In the late '60s during the Vietnam War there was something called the New Left. It had arisen out of the college campuses. It was anti-intellectual and anarchic and totally different from the left of the '30s, the old left which was highly intellectualised. The old left came out of Russia; it had factions depending on people who were pro-Stalinist, pro-Trotskyist.

"I began to think that I could report on 30 years of the life of this country in terms of the dissidence that was expressed on the streets between the '30s and the '60s. But I didn't have a story until I thought of the Rosenbergs. They became the fulcrum for the book, they were the parents from the '30s and there were their children, Daniel and Susan – children of the '60s who had their own problems. The book was never meant to be a documentary because I never knew those people, I only knew what I read in the newspapers. I think of it as a book not about that couple but about the manner in which the whole political system had been directed at these two people. And the idea of what that would feel like and what that would do to the children. It's more a book about the children than about the parents."

But it's a book, I reminded Doctorow, that has powerful resonances today, that seems to contain a lesson. Its criticism of the new left as exemplified by the political vacuity displayed by Daniel surely had parallels with current criticisms of the Occupy Now movement? Within the book Daniel's undirected passion, which seems to mirror the emotional tone of the current Occupy movements, is being contrasted with the ideological rigidity of the older Communism. It is as though we were being told that neither doctrinal rigidity nor free-floating anarchism can provide any radical political solution. Both are as impotent as each other.

"Well, in this country it's usually the fate of radicals to be destroyed," he conceded. "The idea of social security was originally expressed 30 years before it was put into effect by the Roosevelt administration. Meanwhile the fellow who proposed it was accused of sedition and of being a Communist. It's often the effect of the radicals to propose an idea that destroys them, an idea which is nevertheless instituted or installed in society another 20, 30 years later."

So Doctorow resists any idea that he's setting out with any firm moral purpose. So how, I wondered, did he get his ideas for the novels?

Very often, he explained, it's a single image that inspires a whole story. "In *Billy Bathgate* it was a little toy sailboat capsizing in a reservoir and then finding a child dead in the machinery of the waterworks nearby. And I didn't know what those images meant but I just had to pursue them. As you go along the book begins to tell you what it is, and begins to direct you. And the further along you go, so the fewer choices you have. And by the time you get near to the end of it, it's like skiing down a hill."

So he didn't ever know where a book might take him. It somehow develops its own impulsion. He never started with any sense of an ending?

"I never do an outline, I never begin with a grand scheme and I certainly don't write from any sort of aesthetic manifesto that this is the way a novel should be. Every book I've done, I think, has its own voice and depends on the sort of creative accident from which it begins."

And writers are somehow more prone to encounter such creative accidents than others?

"It's hard to explain but there is an endowment that you get from making things up. And this gives you a level of perception or acuity that I don't think you would have if you were simply writing reportage or journalism. Henry James knew about this when he talked about what we do as 'guessing the unseen from the seen'. The slightest little bit of breeze in the air is meaningful to you as a writer. James talks about a damsel being able to write a novel about army life. This young woman who's lived a very sheltered life passes an army barracks and hears a snatch of conversation from the window and if she's a writer goes home and writes a very good novel about army life. And I think that's the way it works. I write about places I've never seen and certainly people I've never met, and it seems to work. I remember Kafka wrote his first novel *America* without ever having left Prague. That's the model for us all, I think."

This almost seemed to suggest that too much reality might not be a blessing to a writer. Facts could get in the way of fiction. But I reminded him of one of his earlier works, *World's Fair*, a book recently selected by *The Guardian* as one of "The Overlooked Classics of American Literature". In this book he seemed determined to impress the reader with the concrete historical reality of the story: its precise correspondence with the facts. "The narrator in *World's Fair* has the same first name as

Doctorow, Edgar," observed Tom Cox in a 2011 article in *The Guardian*. "His father, mother and brother are, like Doctorow's, respectively called Dave, Rose and Donald. When Edgar tells us about his family dog being run over or the magic of the music shop where Dave works, the recollections are so clear and powerfully felt that it seems impossible that these things did not happen to the author himself."

It was, I suggested to Doctorow, as though the characters in this book were engaging in what we'd otherwise think of as a piece of straightforward recollection. They almost seemed to be speaking into a microphone.

"I did that because in the 1980s oral history was something that was coming up rather fast. Studs Terkel was publishing very successful books in which he went around interviewing working people. And there were a lot of other serious academic oral historians at work. And what do we do? We pick up on whatever device will persuade people that they're not reading fiction but actual fact. So I pretended my mother and the other people in my family were talking to a tape recorder. Whereas in fact I was making everything up myself."

In the weeks after my interview with Doctorow I kept finding myself remembering that single-sentence account he'd given of the writer's task, the need to

"pick up on whatever device will persuade people that they're not reading fiction but actual fact". It reminded me of the parallel but quite different writing task that had confronted Michael Frayn when he decided to write a factual biographical account of his childhood that focused on his father: *My Father's Fortune*.

How did a successful novelist like himself manage to keep fiction at bay in such a project? How did he manage to absent himself from such features of his novels as plot and denouement? How could he be sure that his memories had not already become distorted during their familial telling and retelling?

"It certainly is a problem when you try to write an account of anything that's happened in the past, something that you've talked about before. What you remember is your account of it. And when you give that account what you are remembering is the account you gave before. The real problem about trying to reconstruct bits of one's childhood is that they are already the subject of legends, stories one's told oneself and heard other people tell. And to get back to anything that might actually have happened at the beginning is terribly difficult."

I reminded Michael of an article by the neurologist Oliver Sacks I'd read in *The New York Review of Books*. Sacks was writing about how he had started to experience very vivid memories of episodes in his childhood, episodes he'd eventually chronicled in a memoir, *Uncle Tungsten*. Sacks didn't have reliable letters or diaries to verify these events, but he was nonetheless convinced that what he had retained must be valid.

One of the most striking of these memories was of a bomb that fell behind the family house during the Second World War. It was burning with a terrible white-hot heat, and Sacks remembered carrying pails of water, with his brothers, to where his father was trying to put out the blaze with a stirrup pump. But when he mentioned the incident to his older brother, Michael, he was told he couldn't possibly have remembered it. Because he wasn't there. What had actually happened was that his other brother, David, had written a vivid account of the incident in a letter, and the young Oliver had been so enthralled by it that it had become his own memory.

"Although I now know, intellectually," wrote Sacks, "that this memory was 'false', it still seems to me as real, as intensely my own, as before." And he went on to suggest that "all of us 'transfer' experiences to some extent, and at times we are not sure whether an experience was something we were told or read about, even dreamed about, or something that actually happened to us." His conclusion was quite devastating. "There is, it seems, no mechanism in the mind or the brain for ensuring the truth, or at least the veridical character, of our recollections. Memory is dialogic and arises not only from direct experience but from the intercourse of many minds."

So how might Frayn, whose profession relied upon inventing stories, ensure the validity of his memories? Was he aiming to write the literal truth about his father?

"Well, certainly that was my intention insofar as I could research things and look things up in documents." But it hadn't been easy. "There aren't many documents relating to my father's life. He was a salesman, didn't write many letters, didn't get many letters, didn't keep diaries or whatever. He's been long dead, most of the people who knew him are dead. I had to rely mostly on my own recollections. But I certainly tried to make it true."

What prompted him to embark on the memoir? As he got older, was he beginning to see similarities with his father? Was he becoming like him? Was writing about him a form of self-discovery?

"Well, I certainly had this weird feeling that a lot of people have that I sometimes have one of my father's expressions on my face. Not from looking in the mirror. I'd just feel it from inside."

But what really set him off, he explained, was that his own children demanded to know more about their grandparents. "And I began it rather reluctantly. I thought it was going to be rather a pious chore. But of course when you start to think back about the past you do get drawn back into it and I found it a very absorbing and also an extremely emotional experience."

What he found most moving were the small details, such things as his father's use of the phrase "carver's perks" to refer to his habit of placing the best bits of carved chicken on his own plate, a phrase that he later learned was used by his nephew to describe his own habit of preserving the best bits of the Sunday joint for himself.

It was only as he began in a small way to see life from the point of view of his father that Frayn began to realise that he was a remarkable and in some ways a noble man. As a boy he'd had to leave school to support his mother and disabled sister because his own father was a drinker. Then, after he married, he took in his wife's mother, after realising that her husband was as feckless as his own father. Frayn slowly began to realise the struggles his father had to face. In middle age he'd begun to go deaf, a terrible handicap for a man whose livelihood as a salesman depended upon his patter, but he still got up every day and went off to work.

But this new and considerably more appreciative view of his father turned out to be precarious. He told me how amazed he'd been when his sister had declared one day that he'd been a dreadful father. It was a judgement, he thought, that was prompted by his father's extreme reticence, his inability or his unwillingness to talk about his feelings.

But this knowledge, said Frayn, greatly added to the shock of seeing him actually crying when his wife died. Why was he crying so much? His father had a simple but hugely moving answer. "He said, 'Well, look, who's going to miss her most? Me. Me. Because I spent longest with her.'"

So the writing of the memoir did confront Frayn with some painful jolts, some unexpected insights. And also, it made him realise the fundamental connection between this very personal account and his literary work.

"I think with any story, whether it's conscious fiction or whether you're trying to tell the truth," he reflected, "the story to some extent takes over and tells itself. And you have the feeling that characters, after you've laboriously invented them and laboriously thought of some things they might say and do . . . they do seem to start talking themselves. There was a sort of inevitability about these aspects of fiction intruding into any account however much one sought for something called reality.

"I think it goes very deep. I think it's the only way one can think about the world. One has to make sense of the world somehow and one does it through narratives."

Chapter Seven

Making Believe

Alan Ayckbourn – Jonathan Miller – Terry Gilliam

It was a family connection that led to me knowing Alan Ayckbourn long before his first play reached the stage. My wife at the time knew his wife at the time. While I was beginning my academic career as a junior lecturer at the University of York, Alan was down the road working as an assistant producer for BBC Radio Leeds.

None of us had much money to spare so our social life was mostly spent indoors. But this seemed to suit Alan very well. After we'd finished our evening meal we'd all sit around a low table in the front room of his modest estate house in Tadcaster and play games, which, as I remember, were invariably invented by Alan.

His particular favourite was what he called The Word Game. The rules for this were so simple as to be almost non-existent. Each of the four of us was required, in turn, to produce a word, any word at all, and then the remaining three "contestants" were required to produce a one-to-ten critical evaluation of its worth. The winner was the person whose words gained the highest overall score.

So, in a typical round, Alan might ask me for my word. I would produce some such word as "Banana" or "Umbrella". Alan would then lead the adjudication. "'Banana'," he'd muse. "Yes, that's not bad. Not bad at all. That's certainly worth a high seven, perhaps even an eight." The others in the group were then required to give their scores, scores which, in the absence of any discriminating criteria, tended to follow Alan's lead.

So far, so benign. But matters became considerably more

consequential and tense as the round proceeded. "Right, next," Alan would say to his wife, Chris. "Let's have your word."

At such moments in the game Alan's wife would often gently protest that she didn't really know which word to choose because she didn't properly understand the rules. But after some urging from Alan she'd eventually come up with her choice. "Daffodil," she'd offer hesitantly.

She had reason to hesitate, for at this point the game moved up a gear. "Oh, dear, Chris!" Alan would exclaim in the tone of someone coming across an unfortunate accident. "'Daffodil'. 'Daffodil'. That's very poor. Very poor indeed. And such a pity after we'd had such a good start to the game with Laurie's 'Banana'. No, I'm sorry, but I can't go higher than a three. What do you think, Laurie?"

Even though I knew that Alan had just delivered a nonsensical judgement, I somehow felt impelled to play along. "'Daffodil'," I'd muse. "It's not as bad as all that. But still not very good. I really couldn't go beyond a four."

On the way home my wife would rebuke me for playing along with Alan in such a sadistic manner. "Couldn't you see how much your silly game without rules was upsetting Chris?"

Years later when my friendship with Alan had been attenuated by time and place, I'd sit watching one of his wonderful plays in a West End theatre and suddenly recognise not this exact game but a very similar demonstration of how extreme dissonance could be generated in a mundane social setting, and how such dissonance could prompt pain as well as laughter. All that is needed is a little tinkering with reality.

In Ayckbourn's trilogy *The Norman Conquest*, it isn't the subversion of a word game that creates such effects but a displacement of furniture. In that part of the trilogy called *Table Manners*, a lack of the proper chairs for a dinner gathering forces the limp and ineffectual vet, Tom, to accept alternative seating. It's a simple enough device but, as Michael Billington observed in his review of the play in *The Guardian* in 2008, "There are few scenes in modern comedy to rival a fractious family dinner in which tempers are violently lost while the hapless Tom sits on a low-slung chair with head protruding over the table."

Ayckbourn's great skill, a skill that allows Billington in the same review to compare him with Chekhov, is to know how the small frustrations and discomforts caused by matter being even slightly out of place can build into a heightened and even murderous dramatic state.

Although he's always insisted that he doesn't go around with a pencil and notebook looking for such interactional tensions, he somehow seems to find them wherever he goes. In our interview he gave me one example.

"I remember going with my second wife, Heather, and sitting in an Italian restaurant at very tiny tables which were quite close to each other. We'd only just arrived and were busy with menus and first drinks and all of that when I suddenly became aware that the couple opposite us were simply sitting there in absolute silence. I could feel this incredible tension coming off this tiny table. And it transpired that one of them had said something to the other which the other had taken affront at. I was flicking my eyes around and my ears were flapping as I tried to listen for any sound from the silent table. And then as we ordered I heard that man utter this chilling sentence. He leant forward to his partner and he said, 'Do you want me to hit you here or when we get home?'"

Even as he finished the story I could almost sense that Alan was mentally plotting the next scene in this discovered drama. What might happen when the couple did finally get home? How might he manage the shift from restaurant to home on stage?

Alan is endlessly interested in stagecraft: entrances and exits, lighting changes, the arrangement of furniture, the actual shape of the stage. (He so dislikes the proscenium arch that for the London revival of *The Norman Conquests* he insisted upon radically refiguring the entire auditorium of the Old Vic so that he could have his own built-in 'theatre in the round'.) But then, even before he'd written a word, it was just such matters that concerned him when he worked with theatre pioneer Stephen Joseph over 50 years ago.

"I inherited a theatre from a man who had the inspiration to design an exciting space and I then had the experience of working in all sort of branches of theatre: lighting, sound, scenic. All those things. And I was also an actor and a stage manager. All that helped. And the natural progression was to become a director and combining the directing and the writing gave me a lovely control over the material."

Although Alan is happy to talk about the plots of his many plays (at the last count it was 78) he demurs when questions about their meaning arise. He is far more at ease when the conversation turns back to such stagecraft issues as getting people on and off stage, or marking the passing of time.

"It's so easy in film," he explained. "You just move to another shot." But what if, as in one of his early children's plays, you've got a barman who's just been thrown across the room by a woman with supernatural powers, and the next scene is meant to be six months later?

"So I had the barman lying there, and he went, 'Oooh, ooeer, I shan't get up for six months. I'm in terrible agony.' And then the lights change, a couple of blokes come on and say,'Good morning, barman. What a lovely April morning.' I knew that kids could take that information straightaway."

Alan is equally matter-of-fact and craft-centred with his actors. Rather than inviting them to delve deeply into their motivations, he throws out clues to their character: "He's the sort of man who stands in the kitchen and says, 'Darling! The milk's boiling over.'"

But perhaps it is preserving the actor's innocence that is at the top of his agenda.

"You have a read-through and everyone's very nervous. And it's quite quiet. And then you go into the rehearsal room and everyone has a jolly good laugh at all the funny bits. And I let them laugh. Then as we get serious and work on the play, the laughter evaporates and it's never mentioned again, and you can see it cross the actors' minds. 'Oh, yeah, we thought this was funny three or four weeks ago.' But they must still play the line completely guilelessly. I always tell them they must be innocent. And then you watch it again six or seven performances later and the actor's just beginning again to think of it as a laugh line. They begin to shape it slightly. And I think, no, no, keep your innocence."

Alan's concern about the fragility of the comic inevitably reminded me of Howard Jacobson's insistence upon finding the comedy in the language, his refusal to entertain the idea that any great novel, with the honourable exception of *Middlemarch*, could lack humour. I wondered if Alan had the same reaction to the word "comic" or "comedy" being attached to his own calling. Did he mind being a "comedy playwright"? Hadn't he once said that a play without laughs is very much like a flower without water?

"Well, I've thought lately that if you write comic books or plays, you don't expect to be taken seriously until the humour has long ceased to be funny. Once the tide's gone out and all you've got left is the glum subtext, they'll say, 'Oh, these are very interesting plays.'"

It was as though there was something wrong with laughter, it was somehow an inferior emotion.

"Yes. I had a review once for *Bedroom Farce* and it said, 'I laughed shamelessly.' That was put up as a quote, and I thought ,'Why are you ashamed of laughing?' As though we are laughing at things we shouldn't be laughing at. A man once said to me as he came out of the theatre, and it's one of the nicest compliments I've ever had: 'I'll tell you something. I wouldn't have laughed at that if I'd known I was laughing at the time.' That's great. As he was leaving the theatre he thought, 'Hang on, I shouldn't have been laughing.'"

It is, no doubt, all part of the categorising imperative that just as one of our most significant playwrights can find himself bracketed as a mere writer of middle-class comedies, so one of our most astute theatre and opera directors, Jonathan Miller, can be dismissed as an "intellectual" – or, in one of the most pejorative terms in the English critical vocabulary, "over-intellectual".

But, as I quickly discovered when I began to talk to Jonathan about his approach to directing actors, he had as little time as Ayckbourn for deep theoretical Stanislavskian investigations of a character's motives and background. What mattered, just as with Ayckbourn, was to keep them innocent, to remind them of what they knew all along but had forgotten. In his words, to remind them "to abstain from dramatic clichés and to undertake to perform the overlooked and the negligible".

A good example, he told me, was an exchange with a diva when he was directing *The Marriage of Figaro*. "There's that famous aria in the third act where the Countess sits and meditates about how awful her life is. And the diva said, 'Well, where do I stand?' And I said, 'Well, you can't possibly stand, you're actually in a state of depression. You would sit in a chair, as I'm sitting now, staring sightlessly out into the middle distance.' And she said, 'Well, what do I do with my hands?' And I said, 'What an absurd question.' I said, 'You don't have to ring up a hand centre at half-past seven in the morning and say, "What am I going to do with my hands, I mean when I'm not actually using them to sew or drink with?"' I said, 'Do what we always do.'"

He explained that he was very much inspired by the work of an Australian philosopher, Brian O'Shaughnessy, who drew his attention to the idea of sub-intentional movements. "You're doing it now," he pointed out to me. "You're moving your hand across your lips. So I said to her, 'While you're thinking just doodle with the tip of your index finger . . .' And at the end of it she said, 'The funny thing is I've been able to sing that aria for the first time properly.' And I said, 'That's because you're using it in order to express something which is real, rather than being an opera singer.'" What one has to concentrate upon is what is interesting. "And most of the interesting things are the negligible."

But how, I wondered, can he take that approach with a great tragedy like *King Lear*, which he has produced five times? Surely a concentration on small details would trivialise the drama? "I cannot bear the heroic," he responded staunchly. "He's a sort of negligible figure, King Lear. A silly old man who tries to get the attention of his youngest daughter. . ." And, he explained, this obsession with Cordelia to the exclusion of the other two daughters – the real key to the plot and Lear's downfall – can be conveyed in the simplest of stage directions. He must keep his eyes on Cordelia, and take no notice of the extravagant blandishments of her sisters.

I wondered how much this emphasis on the negligible, the small gestures and movements, the minutiae of social interaction, derived from Miller's medical background. "Well, you see, I think that you've gone to the heart of the matter really," he agreed at once. He remembered that during his training he was introduced to clinical methods. "And most of that is to do with history-taking, listening to people, listening to the way in which they express their symptoms. But also having an eye for the negligible detail which gives the game away."

And this, he agreed, is a technique that has stayed with him, connecting his work as a director with his medical training and also, perhaps most importantly, with his interest in neurology. "I was interested in disorders of action, disorders of perception and disorders of language," he explained. "And where better to study it than with people who had deficiencies in that respect? So that undoubtedly I was trained in the hospital to pay attention to those details, but my interest in those details probably had developed much earlier on."

And clearly his hatred of the exaggerated, the over-dramatic, derives from his belief that "great art dignifies the negligible and says, that's all there is, pay attention to it, pay attention." In this, I suggested, he echoes the work of the American sociologist Erving Goffman, whose books are all concerned with the fascinating topic of micro-management.

Miller agreed that Goffman was an important influence, as was the Oxford philosopher J. L. Austin, who wrote an essay on pretending. "Austin goes into minute linguistic detail about the varieties of pretence and at what point a pretence becomes real and what it is about a pretence that makes it different from the real," he said. Austin's analysis of the different excuses people use to account for their behaviour certainly influenced Goffman, as well as the Berkeley philosopher John Searle, whom Miller also admires.

"Searle coined the notion of 'the speech act'. What are you trying to do by means of this particular utterance? Now Searle was in fact a student of Austin, so we have a trio of people who've had a profound influence on my approach to the theatre." And one of the most important effects of this influence is on Miller's approach to language. He shortened the length of *Long Day's Journey Into Night* by an hour and 15 minutes, for example, simply by having the characters interrupt each other as people do in a family.

"They just don't listen to each other," he said. "Or they do listen to each other because they pick up the few words they need to and then go on. If you listen to people talking they overlap. I remember when I was doing *Long Day's Journey*. As always the actors came in with their part highlighted in yellow. And I had to explain to them very early on, I said, 'Well, listen, I'm afraid that during those yellow parts, when you're talking, there'll be grey parts when the other people are talking at the same time. And that's part of the decorum of conversation now ... I mean there are little, tiny unnoticed things.'"

Miller's method, his reliance on the subtle and the negligible, could hardly on the face of it be more different from that of the flamboyant, darkly surrealist film director Terry Gilliam. Originally best known for his anarchic animations for *Monty Python's Flying Circus*, he went on to establish a formidable reputation for such memorably disturbing films as *Brazil*, *12 Monkeys* and *Fear and Loathing in Las Vegas* – and more recently he directed critically acclaimed productions of *The Damnation of Faust* and *Benvenuto Cellini*. He doesn't shy away from the dramatic, the shocking, the exaggerated – indeed he relishes them all. And yet there are some striking similarities between his imagination, his approach to story-telling, and those of Jonathan Miller.

Like Miller, for example, he is fascinated by the ways children see the world, and that is what he seeks to recapture in his films. He told me that while the recent remake of *King Kong* was technically impressive, it was the original, with its makeshift puppet and primitive effects, that engaged him more.

"In the original I think I'm seeing magic because I'm seeing a trick and I don't know quite how it's done and that makes it fantastic," he said. "In the new version, I don't even know there's a trick going on." But wasn't this a trifle disingenuous, given the extraordinary effects Gilliam achieves in his own films? How, for example, did he manage to produce the flying sequences with Jonathan Pryce in *Brazil*?

That, he insisted, was a matter of luck and made his point for him. After all, the whole rather amateur rigging could easily have gone wrong. The trick could have failed. "Let's start with that painted cloud background," he began. "In front of that we built these big clouds out of chicken wire on frames covered with kapok, the stuff which is probably in this chair right now. And then in front of that we built these tanks with dry ice in them which we pumped steam through. So you've got those shapes back there giving it depth and you've got this steam dry ice creating clouds. So when you add in a little model of Jonathan Pryce with only a wingspan of action-man size, you can watch his wings flapping through all this stuff in a way that creates movement and is surprising every time."

It sounded as though it could so easily have gone wrong – but that seemed almost like an incidental bonus. "Nature is full of surprises," he told me happily. "Most film-making now is trying to get nature out of the process so that the computer and those who make the programmes have complete control. That's terrifying, because directors by nature want to control everything that happens. The way it's going now, there's too much control given to the director, and not to things that happen.

"I've got the technical knowledge and skill to do pretty much anything, but it's boring now. So when something goes wrong, when an earthquake occurs in the middle of the shot – ooh! I'm alive again!"

And, like both Miller and Ayckbourn, Gilliam insists he is first and foremost a craftsman – rather like his father, who was a carpenter. "Yeah. Craftsmanship is what it's all about," he agreed. "These things, hands – you build things, physical things." And, he thinks, it's this emphasis on craft that inspires him. "It's playing," he reflects. "It's not imagination, I think it's play. It's like what a child does and that's why I've clung desperately to this childlike ability to play with things . . . Everything conspires to suppress that childhood ability to reinvent the world at every moment, to ensure that when that door opens, the next time it opens on to another place.

"What I love," he enthused, "is the time in the morning when you're half asleep lying in bed and there's a point when your senses are not quite functioning. Smell may be working but as you wake up so you see things – oh, that's what it looks like; oh, that's what it feels like; that's what it sounds like; this is what it smells like. And as each of these senses come to play that world becomes a concrete thing. And I love that moment, the moment before it becomes concrete."

And maybe this dreamlike state is close to the sensation of creating new worlds. "There's a moment that occurs that still thrills me when it happens," he told me. "I start doing a storyboard. We've written the scene. There it is and I don't look at it and I just start drawing it and it changes because [of] this weird thing when you draw – ooh, an image comes in, a shape comes in, a colour. And I've shifted the scene way over here by several degrees. Then I go back to the script and adjust the script to my storyboard. So it's this ongoing relationship between what this imagination or whatever it is – and the reality."

Tireless in his pursuit of ideas that excite and challenge him, he must, I wondered, be at least bemused that by far and away his most financially successful work is the children's film *Time Bandits*. Surely he'd rather be remembered for his darker, more ambitious achievements?

He finds comfort in an example from his profession. "Ken Russell produced some of the most extraordinary films. His films made me crazy because one minute there were the most brilliant, beautiful, sensual, intelligent things going on. And then the next, the most juvenile nonsense. But it didn't matter, it was the great moments that made up for the nonsense.

"And that's what I want," he concluded. "I want moments. I want to make movies that have one moment that actually hooks itself in some poor kid's brain and is with him for the rest of his life."

Part Three
Family and Friends

Chapter Eight

Growing Pains

John Lydon – Peter Hitchens – Christopher Hitchens

In these post-Freudian days, people of accomplishment are required to pay special attention to their childhood. They are expected, for the benefit of themselves and their curious public, to construct personal histories that throw some light upon the nature of their current fame. "Both writers and readers are inclined to make the childhood emblematic of the already known adult achievement," observed the novelist Jenny Diski in a 2013 article in the *London Review of Books*. "Either as something to overcome – poverty, abuse, no education – or as a period of unwitting training for whatever they came to do so well or so badly later on."

I was, of course, interested in the stories that my celebrity guests had to tell about their childhood but the knowledge that they were likely to have told very much the same story in other places meant that I was anxious to question or even disrupt some of these well-rehearsed narratives, even to suggest that what had always been paraded as a happy or an unhappy home might be otherwise.

But there were still some occasions when the childhood seemed properly emblematic, when its association with the fame that was to follow made such good if complex sense that I had no wish to do anything that might break the link.

Such was the case with John Lydon. When I mentioned to friends that I was going to talk with the man who'd achieved fame as the lead singer of the Sex Pistols back in the late '70s, they assumed that I'd been solely attracted by his capacity for arousing moral outrage. But in fact I had another and rather calmer reason. Of course I'd been fascinated by his early career, but I'd also been listening to some of the songs Lydon had written for Public Image Ltd, the band he'd founded after leaving the Pistols in 1978, and been struck by their lyricism and their imagery.

John Lydon: "A masterpiece of annoyance"

In a song called "No Bird", for example, he'd used some wonderfully precise words to capture and gently satirise a suburban idea of the perfect life, a heaven characterised by "shallow spreads of ordered lawns" and "mild-mannered mews" patrolled by "well-intentioned rules". He'd also written most movingly about the death of his mother from cancer in a song he called "Death Disco".

What was there in his childhood that could explain both his extraordinary capacity to shock and his poetic sensibility? He'd warned me before we sat down to talk that he had no wish to expose himself, and his anxiety about the whole occasion became very evident when we were all forced to wait nearly an hour for him to arrive on the set because he'd cut himself quite severely with a razor as he was getting ready. "That's obviously a sign of nerves, isn't it?" he said as he sat down before me, "and if you weren't nervous you wouldn't be human. This is a life performance for me." A moment later he was busy throwing up his guard. "I'm not a fool. I'm not going to reveal all my secrets . . . if you're that open, that honest, you're really rather stupid."

But I had a quotation ready that I thought might open the gate. "You said once, 'I don't sing, walk, talk or look like anyone else.' How much was that sense of difference derived from the time in childhood when you'd been so desperately ill, so close to death, with meningitis?"

He slowly told me the story, told me how as a seven-year-old he'd somehow believed that what he'd had to endure was his own fault. But most of all he told me about the extraordinary loss of memory that had resulted from the hospital treatment he'd received. When he was ready to go home he was unable to recognise even his own parents. They were "two complete strangers". But "I had to believe these were my mum and dad. They were kind. They seemed to want me. And the hospital seemed not to want me. I had no place else to go. It was murderously cruel and tortuous to me because I thought inside that it must all be my fault. I must have done something wrong. It was the Catholic guilt they drive into you at a very early age."

So severe was his loss of memory that his mother had to sit down with him and start all over from scratch. At the age of seven he had to relearn the alphabet. "To this day I couldn't tell you the alphabet in any order. I still don't know it. It gets really confused after 'M'. And my mind goes blank and bored trying to count past ten."

His treatment also left him with a curved spine, incredibly weak eyes and a proneness to epileptic seizure. But although he was not anxious to talk for too long about this part of his childhood, he was only too happy to embrace every one of these childhood inflictions as a certain sign of his difference. He told me he found it "entertaining" when critics of the Pistols called him Quasimodo or Richard the Third. "That was not an insult to me at all." He would never have wanted it to be otherwise. "It's ultimately a reward. I think it set me off better than I would have been originally. I might have grown up to be a really boring little turd instead of a masterpiece of annoyance."

If I hadn't reckoned that any such theoretical speculation would have been instantly kicked into touch, I might at this point have suggested to John that his story was a perfect case study of Adlerian compensation theory, of the manner in which those suffering from some sort of "organ inferiority" (in Adler's own case it was childhood rickets) strive with particular intensity to assert their place in the world. I might even have gone further and suggested that Lydon's time as Johnny Rotten, his capacity in that persona for generating excitement and a sense of danger in his audience, had close affinities with the character type that Adler attributed to those who "pathologically" over-compensate for their disabilities: "Their movements will have to have a certain grandiose gesture about them. They seek to secure their position in life with extraordinary efforts, with greater haste and impatience, with more intense impulses, without consideration of any one else," Adler wrote in a 1927 article. "Through these exaggerated movements toward their exaggerated goal of dominance these children become more noticeable, their attacks on the lives of others necessitate that they defend their own lives. They are against the world, and the world is against them."

This may be a dramatic characterisation but Adler's words do seem to capture the extreme bravery, the intensity with which John lived during the time of the Sex Pistols. He told me a little of that life. "The way we used to perform was that we'd just get in a Transit van and go off, go off up north. And that could be really dangerous. Just the four of us and maybe occasionally one or two others. But them northern clubs. I mean they hated the south with a major passion. And there'd be three hundred really vicious purpose-filled yobs wanting to kill the cockneys. Fantastic. What an upbringing. And we managed to win them over. You know, if you've got the bottle to stand in front of that kind of hate and persevere and finally push on through, you've won respect. You know that's the stuff of champions. It's not 'I want to be a rock star, Mummy. And look, Daddy's bought me a guitar.'"

John Lydon's story is, of course, also a classic example of childhood being used as something to be overcome so that the real persona, the talented adult, can emerge. At the opposite extreme, as Diski observed, is the view of childhood as "a period of unwitting training" for later achievements. It was the prospect of examining this perspective that most appealed when I knew that I would be interviewing both Christopher Hitchens and his younger brother Peter, two people who shared a childhood but went on to hold diametrically opposed political and cultural ideologies.

I was glad that the filming schedule meant that I would be talking to Peter several months before his brother, even though news of the seriousness of Christopher's illness meant that there was some uncertainty as to whether he might be well enough to talk to me on the American date we had in the diary.

It is customary among left liberals to dismiss Peter Hitchens as not much more than a right-wing rabble-rouser whose proper place is in the columns of *The Mail on Sunday* or in the chair reserved for controversialist on such programmes as *Any Questions* and *Question Time*. But this is too glib. Peter Hitchens is far from being in hock to any political party or any recognisable ideological persuasion. Although his traditional, some would say archaic, views on divorce, homosexuality and sex before marriage have earned him widespread opprobrium, he is never ready to compromise.

Here is how he described his reputation in a *Guardian*

interview: "I know a lot of people consider me to be disreputable or foaming at the mouth, but you have to learn not to care, or at least not to mind. I don't like being called 'bonkers' . . . but I take comfort from the fact that most totalitarian regimes tend to classify their opponents as mentally disordered." One suspects that it was this bravery in the face of extreme hostility that played some part in the controversial decision to award Peter the Orwell Prize in 2010. Although the prize was nominally for his foreign reporting, there were those who could not forget his political perspective. Nick Cohen, the *Observer* columnist, railed against the judges: "How dare Peter Hitchens be nominated for the Orwell Prize by all these scummy, useless old people? Don't rob the grave of poor Orwell." Peter was hardly perturbed by such outbursts. On receipt of the award he mildly observed, "I'm quite surprised all you lefties have given me the prize."

I knew that Peter and Christopher had been brought up in a solidly bourgeois home. I'd also read that Peter had greatly admired and respected his father, who'd been a career naval officer. But knowing Peter's reputation for contrariness I was not too surprised to find that right from the beginning of our interview he was happily at work confounding my expectations. "You were proud of your naval father when you were growing up? You respected him?" I suggested.

"I think it would be dishonest of me to claim that that was so then. I think my relations with my parents during that period were pretty bad. And while in later life I've learned to think a good deal better of my parents and a good deal less well of myself, at that time, that awful time of self-indulgence, the early teens and early adolescence, I thought so well of myself that I thought quite badly of my parents. So no, it wouldn't be true to say that at that time I had much respect for them. I was horrible to them."

But was he ever able to express such lack of respect? I also had an idea of his family home as one where it was difficult to express opinions let alone emotions.

"I think everybody thinks their upbringing is pretty well normal and then they find out later that other people had quite different childhoods. There are things I now know that I didn't know at the time because my parents thought it was their job to keep them from me. Their marriage wasn't particularly happy. My father had been pretty disappointed with his life after the Navy beached him after Suez in 1956. And he found himself doing things he didn't particularly want to do in places he didn't particularly want to be and paying to send me to expensive schools, which I didn't actually much want to go to. And all that was going on. But half of it I wasn't aware of. I was totally insensitive to my parents' problems at the time. And it shocks me now to realise how utterly insensitive I was to what was going on."

But, I suggested, this was hardly his fault. It seemed that nobody spoke about their problems or their concerns in the Hitchens household. I reminded him of a TV programme in which he'd agreed to escort the interviewer around the family home. He'd apparently halted at one upstairs door and said, "Well, this is the parents' bedroom. We never went anywhere near there." Peter nodded as he remembered the occasion. "Well, yes. Again it's difficult to explain in this much more relaxed age how quite different it was then. I grew up technically in the 1950s. But to all intents and purposes, it was the 1930s. My childhood would have been much more recognisable to a child of 1930 that it would be to a child of 2011. Or indeed a child of 1993. It was quite old-fashioned. It was more reserved. It was cooler. There wasn't all that much conversation between parent and child. And we were away a lot of the time as well. Boarding school started at seven. So for a large chunk of the year I simply wasn't there."

But wasn't there some schooltime compensation to be found in the company of his brother?

"It's always difficult to explain this. Some people get on

enormously well with their siblings and remain friends throughout their lives, some people absolutely cannot stand their siblings and never speak to them for decade on decade. We, at that stage, simply didn't get on. There were two and a half years' difference between us."

"You were the younger?"

"Yes, and given that we attended, for quite a lot of the time, the same boarding school, that is an enormous gulf. Because even when you were at home together, you'd know that you'd soon be back at school with its very strict gradations of age. Remember, this was a school where I didn't know the Christian names of the other pupils. We didn't use them. It was only surnames. And the difference between one year and the next was as rigid as the Indian caste system. You just didn't deal with people in the year above or the year below. And yet I had a brother in the same school, a brother I knew from home, someone I knew more about than anybody else at the school, but I could barely speak to him or see him."

"But then," I pressed him, "when you did see each other at home, when you were able to speak to each other, you apparently spent almost all the time arguing? Why?"

"His explanation, as far as I can discover, is that he was going on fine until I arrived. You know this thing about children. They're told that Mummy and Daddy have brought a new brother home from hospital and the response of the child who's in situ is to say, 'Great, when are you taking him back?' And I suspect that was Christopher's attitude to me. There he was doing fine and suddenly this new person arrived and took away some of the attention that he thought was rightfully his."

And these constant arguments about everything and nothing were not just verbal jousting?

"Oh, no. There was fighting. He pretended not to be hurt. I would get over his back and pound heavily on his back with my tiny fists and he would claim that it didn't hurt. I can absolutely assure you that it did. I was putting a lot of force into it."

Matters got so out of hand between the brothers that their parents drew up a peace treaty between them. This treaty, called The Treaty of Cedarwood after the name of the family home, was then hung on the wall in the hope that it would secure a lasting truce. It didn't.

I suggested to Peter that the intensity of the battling and his failure to remember its basis in reality would suggest to a vulgar Freudian that there was a simple explanation at hand. Both brothers were competing for the attention and love of their mother. Peter waved away the suggestion.

"Well, it's always possible, isn't it. But that's the kind of thing vulgar Freudians say."

Almost as soon as I began to talk to Christopher Hitchens in his roomy Washington flat, I asked about his version of those childhood days. Was he any better than Peter at remembering the basis of their constant disagreements? At that age they could hardly have been arguing about politics or religion.

"Until his arrival," Christopher explained, "I'd had things more or less arranged as I wanted them. Namely, the whole attention of my mother. The possibility of marrying her. The possibility of elbowing her husband out of the picture one way or another. Supreme power. This plan did not take into account the arrival of a sibling who was born slightly too near . . . He was too near to be a baby brother needing protection. But near enough to be a rival. And smart and tough."

So he would not disagree with the argument that they were both competing for a mother's love? Would he wave away any such a suggestion as his brother had appeared to do?

"Oh, no. It's quite wrong to wave away a thing like that. It's not waveable away."

And how intense was that competition for the mother?

"I'm sure I can remember telling him that he was adopted . . .

with a reasonable chance that he might believe it."

Although I was smugly pleased to have Christopher's confirmation of my Freudian theory about the origin of their childhood arguments, I did not want to go on and commit the reductionist error of believing that their arguments in later life rested on the same biographical foundations.

Christopher did not hold his strong views on secularism and socialism in order to contradict the religious and political sentiments espoused by his brother. Or vice versa. Both brothers argued their cases with intelligence and passion. But it was difficult, I suggested to Peter, not to find something slightly comic in the diametrically opposed nature of their beliefs. Consider their views on the Iraq invasion. Anyone familiar with the predominantly conservative political stance taken by Peter on such matters as homosexuality, divorce, feminism and global warming might assume that he would favour the invasion, in much the same way that those who knew of Christopher's long-standing opposition to all forms of American imperialism would predict his whole-hearted opposition to the attempt to depose Saddam Hussein. But as it turned out Peter was totally opposed to the invasion while Christopher openly sided with President Bush. You could, I suggested to Peter, understand why some observers of the quarrel might be inclined to put it down to contrariness rather than deeply held beliefs.

Peter immediately reproved me. "You have to pay more attention. We do actually develop our opinions separately, and they are entirely logical. He's a much more intelligent interpreter of left-wing utopianism than most of his coevals and as a result he very rapidly worked out what I worked out as well, that the Kosovo war, which I also opposed, and the Iraq war are left-wing wars. That's why I'm against them. And that's why he's for them."

Did Christopher also recognise that there could be something almost comic in the manner in which they constantly seemed to be standing on opposite sides of the fence? Perhaps, I suggested, we should look for an affinity between them, not in terms of the positions they adopted but in terms of the absolute certainty with which they maintained them. Did he recognise what I called "a complementary intolerance of ambiguity"?

"Yes, I do. Because I've noticed that . . . we often find the same kinds of politicians repulsive. Often for slightly different reasons. But there's the same feeling. How can anyone look at, say, Bill Clinton, without realising you're dealing with a dangerous sort of phony? A hopeless case of narcissism. Why would anyone volunteer to help – be proud to help – pump up this already bloated ego? I didn't know what he [Peter] thought about it until I'd published my own stuff. He's good on things like that. As he is, for example, on the wretched church of which he's a member. He understands as easily as I do that Rowan Williams [the former Archbishop of Canterbury] does this perfect impersonation of a Welsh sheep trapped, bleating, on some hillside in the rain."

Christopher and Peter did share one thing from their youth: at one time, before Peter found religion, they were both members of the Trotskyist International Socialists. But although Peter's ideology changed dramatically, Christopher detected a constancy about the setting in which such ideology was expressed. He wasn't simply a member of the Church of England. That wouldn't be Trotskyist enough. Peter, he pointed out, "could only be a member of the Church of England on the condition that he's a member of the most extreme, isolated, derided opposition group within it."

When I now look back at my interviews with Peter and Christopher Hitchens I notice how much time I seem to have spent trying to root out the basis of their antagonism, trying to elicit some degree of agreement and mutual respect.

I recognise now that this was at least partly impelled by my knowledge of Christopher's condition, by my recognition that probably within months of my talking to him he would succumb to the oesophageal cancer that had, in his own words, already made him "a prisoner of chemotherapy".

In my quest to find some ground for a reconciliation between the two, I turned to George Orwell. Christopher had written a book on the great man and in a *Vanity Fair* article had characterised his significance.

"By declining to lie even as far as possible to himself, and by his determination to seek elusive but uncomfortable truth, he showed how much can be accomplished by an individual who unites the qualities of intellectual honesty and moral courage."

Was this evaluation shared by Peter? He had, after all, been awarded the Orwell Prize, so might this have been the occasion when he expressed rather similar sentiments to his brother, even though Orwell, by most reckonings, stood well to the left of Peter in terms of political convictions?

I only had to look as far as Peter Hitchens' blog in the *Mail Online*. "Because Orwell was of the left (though a very troubled and troublesome member of that movement) he is regarded by many on the left as their perpetual property," he wrote, just one week after receiving the award. "I disagree. I think Orwell belongs to the truth, not the left."

"Presumably," I said to Peter, "this is what you admire about your brother. Because although he's speaking a different truth from yours, he is speaking it unambiguously. He's speaking it with a great degree of literacy and force. He's got very little time for grubby little ideologies."

Although I was already far enough into the interview to know that Peter had a built-in dislike of concurring, this struck home.

Yes, he conceded. The antagonism between them was not as it had been in the past. There was this mutual recognition. Somehow they could not get the old familiar arguments off the ground any more. "We were supposed to have a public debate about religion. It was a complete flop for reasons I won't trouble you with."

They couldn't work up a proper disagreement?

"It was the business of going over to the States and seeing him before the debate. I felt that the quarrel . . . our quarrel was over."

His parents, I suggested, would have been pleased to hear it.

"You know, if I could have found the Treaty of Cedarwood I would have put it back on the wall."

But I knew that this lack of an ability or inclination to quarrel any more wasn't the only surprising thing about this meeting. Christopher, I reminded him, actually cooked him dinner?

"Yeah. Astonishing. He cooked a nice dinner. You might as well expect to find Mick Jagger playing Crown Green Bowls."

Chapter Nine

Dutiful Daughters?

Kathy Burke – Cleo Laine – Miriam Margolyes – Lucinda Lambton

It says something for the staying power of shame that I can still recall the moment when I grumbled about the prospect of interviewing someone I now regard as an exceptionally talented and utterly honest actor, writer and director.

"We're in luck," said the producer when he rang about forthcoming interviews. "We've managed to book Kathy Burke."

Kathy Burke. I said the name to myself again. Kathy Burke. Yes, it rang a bell. But not loudly enough. "Tell me more," I said.

"You know, Waynetta Slob. 'I am smoking a fag.' That was her catchphrase."

An image came into my mind. A very distinct image. An unfortunate image.

"I'm not quite sure about this one," I told my producer. "Would she be able to generate an interesting conversation?"

"Of course."

"Waynetta Slob?"

"No, not Waynetta Slob. Kathy Burke. *The* Kathy Burke. She's completely brilliant. She's got a BAFTA for Best Actress in that Gary Oldman film, *Nil by Mouth*. Don't you remember her in that? Fantastic. And she was in that film about a girls' Borstal. *Scrubbers*. And then she went on from being a successful actor to being a fine writer and director."

Of course. Of course, I knew all that but somehow I hadn't been able to rid myself of the belief that it was Waynetta and not Kathy that I was being invited to interview. In my head Waynetta still lived.

My starting point in the interview was her childhood. I knew already that this had been difficult, even tragic. Her mother had died when she was still a baby and she was then taken in by a neighbour and only returned home to her two brothers and her drunken father when she was nine years old. It sounded such a sad, dysfunctional family story. How did she cope when she finally got back home?

"I had more freedom. Dad wasn't really around. Dad, you know, had this bad drink problem." Her brothers did their best to look after her, but she was often left to her own devices. "I remember doing a lot of walking on my own and being on my own and I liked that, actually."

I wondered if she was speaking too casually about her father's drunkenness. Wasn't it a bit more than "a drink problem"? I'd heard that he took out his drunken rages on his children.

"Yeah, he could do. He could do. I mean, you know, he was really fucked up with it at times. But there were times when he'd have months of sobriety. But then that was tricky, because now he was trying to be, you know, the rule master and laying down the law, and it's like, well, one minute you're here saying all that and then the next minute you're off for weeks and we don't see you."

But even that, she said, had its advantages. "I am a bit of a rebel and a little bit of an anarchist – I mean, I look back and I think I probably liked it when Dad was off. Do you know what I mean? I could just get on with my own thing."

And it wasn't as if the children took their father's tyrannical outbursts all that seriously. "I would do things to my dad that my brothers wouldn't dare," she recalled, referring to one particularly memorable prank when she made him look like Hitler. "It was in the days of Brylcreem, so when Dad was, you know, comatosed basically from the booze, then I'd comb his hair down and get a bit of coal from the fire and put that on and he'd be lying there like that, and we'd just be in hysterics."

So from early on she discovered she had the ability to make people laugh: the first of all her defence mechanisms and the key to later success. When she was a little girl, did her friends know that her father was an alcoholic?

"Well, they would have known because I did impressions of Dad, but that's how they would know . . . I do this drunk Irishman."

As Kathy talked, I realised how she had sidestepped so many of the familiar psychological truisms about childhood. Here was a young girl without a mother, living at home with a drunken dad, and yet never once during our interview did she invoke any of the familiar deprivation clichés. She not only found ways to handle her difficult father, she found an effective substitute. She told me that the dad she always wished she'd had was from the TV.

"Yes, no disrespect to my dad, especially as in the last years of his life he really sorted himself out, but Eric Morecambe. I mean there was so much energy in the man. All he wanted to do was make you laugh. I just found him uplifting and beautiful and my heart broke when had his heart attack."

It also struck me during this interview that despite all the vicissitudes that Kathy had endured – she also told me in graphic medical detail about how as an adult she'd nearly died because of a hospital failure to detect an abnormality in the functioning of her adrenal glands – she had remained very true to her background. Not through any conscious effort on her part. She simply seemed incapable of putting on any airs, of assuming the smallest of graces.

I was fascinated to see if any such fidelity to childhood roots was discernible in Cleo Laine. It was perhaps a sentimental legacy of my teenage crush on her that I rather liked to believe that she'd been required to forget or disguise some aspects of her past in order to fit in so readily alongside her husband John Dankworth, a man so laid back, so cool, that he'd once been memorably described as "couth, kempt and shevelled".

Was her childhood in Southall quiet and reserved?

"Oh, no. I was the middle child and when my brother was born my nose was completely out of joint. It's a myth of the family that I said – I couldn't have said it because I was only 18 months old when he was born – anyway the myth is that I said, 'We don't want him. Put him under the bed.'"

And it wasn't only the appearance of a new brother that prompted family arguments.

"Oh, I love argument. That was our family tradition. My father argued continually with my mother and they threw things at each other. I loved all that."

"But did you go on arguing when you married John? Or did you have to repress that part of you?"

She paused a moment before delivering her verdict.

"John grew to love it," she said firmly.

"Because he had to learn to love it?"

"He had to. He had to argue. Although my daughter Jacqui remembers that we were arguing one time and he just got up, got into the car, and drove off, because he couldn't stand it any more. But I love arguments."

No one could accuse the present-day Cleo Laine of being in any way cautious about expressing her feelings, but I enjoyed watching how talking about her family seemed to make her more animated. And this was particularly evident when the subject was her father.

He was Jamaican, while Cleo's mother was white – at a time when mixed marriages were frowned upon. "My mother must have been a feminist of the highest order – because to have married a black man in the '20s. . ." So she admired her mother greatly. But she was even closer to her father. She inherited his drive, his insistence on doing things his own way, and most of all his talent.

"He was a wonderful singer, but he never became a professional except that he used to busk and I didn't know anything about that until much later when I realised what those piles of pennies on the kitchen table were."

And what he sang were the standard hits of the day. "Pennies From Heaven", she remembered, was a big favourite of his. "And just before he died I went to see him," she recalled. "And we sang it as a duet, 'Pennies From Heaven'."

Her father was, she told me with some glee, an eccentric man. "He used to dress like Anthony Eden with the hat, the striped trousers and so on," she remembered. "I think he had pretensions of some sort or other. And he rode a bicycle all over Southall with a pipe hanging from his mouth. He was known for that."

He was also known as a ranter. "He'd go to Hyde Park and stand on a box and rant and rave there," she said, though she didn't know what on earth he ranted about. During the Depression, when it was difficult to get work and virtually impossible for a black man, he'd spend his time tinkering, making things. Both her parents, she remembered, used to make ice-cream. "He used to put the tub on his bike and travel down to Runnymede and that's where we learned how to swim. Because he threw us in."

He was a quick-tempered man, something she was eager to excuse. "I call Jamaica 'the belligerent island' because for some reason or other they're – they're belligerent people, you know, they stick up for their rights."

Kathy Burke and Cleo Laine shared a very working class background. And although there were so many differences between their families it was difficult not to regard their achievements as very much of their own doing. Both had been helped by others outside the family – Kathy regularly cited the huge influence of her drama teacher, Anna Scher – but neither had been exactly cosseted, kept away from those tough, awkward aspects of life that might have impinged upon their burgeoning artistic talents.

Timothy Anderson

Miriam Margolyes: "I'm upset if people don't notice me."

Enter Miriam Margolyes, now probably one of the most readily recognised stage and screen character actors in the English-speaking world. She's been in countless films and plays, performed three different roles in the TV comedy *Blackadder*, starred in the musical *Wicked*, played Professor Sprout in the Harry Potter films and received widespread acclaim for her tribute to Dickens's women. And Miriam told me that, in her childhood, her Jewish parents had positively "smothered" their only child in love, almost to the point of suffocation.

She looked up to her father, a gentle, modest physician. But without a doubt the biggest influence in her life was her large, pushy, extrovert, demanding mother: a woman who left school at 14, had overriding ambitions for her only daughter and was, I suggested, just a tad, well, vulgar. "Yes, I think she probably was, actually," Miriam agreed. "But she had such vitality that I never saw that part until later. I mean, I'm looking at her now through the prism of age which is a distorting influence on me as well and I'm also seeing her through the eyes perhaps of those around me.

She was big, she was fat, she was loud, she was warm, she was caustic and she was embarrassing."

Embarrassing how?

"When we went to people's houses, you know, she'd pick up the plate and look at the back of it and say, 'Oh, Doulton,' you know. And she'd say, 'You can get £15 for that!' She would price everything and I think that is perhaps a little vulgar and I do that. So I'm vulgar, too!"

They were also both rather pushy. That pushiness was how Miriam came to model for Augustus John. She'd seen him interviewed on television and decided she'd like to meet him. So at the age of 17 she wrote to him offering to model – for nothing. She didn't realise at the time that nothing would mean – wearing nothing. "And for some reason my parents allowed me to do it. I'll never know why they did."

Perhaps they did because this experience meshed with her mother's vaunting ambitions for her. At the time she was posing in the nude for Augustus John, her mother decided that Miriam should go to Cambridge. And, naturally, she enlisted the help of the country's most distinguished intellectual: Isaiah Berlin.

"Well, the thing was Mummy was pushy for those she loved," she explained. "She was pushy for me, for my father. She wasn't really pushy for herself. She wanted me to succeed with all her heart and, in a way, perhaps I have. I don't know if she would think that I'm now where I should be. But she asked Isaiah Berlin, who was a patient of my father's, if he would support my application for college entrance and of course he did."

Such nerve would be astonishing in anyone, but particularly, perhaps, in a woman who had had no real education. How did her mother know that this was somebody who could open every intellectual door?

"She knew, she was shrewd," Miriam told me. "She had her ear to the ground in that way and she immediately knew this was the man to ask and so, of course, no college would turn me down. It wasn't that I was bright – it was she who was bright."

Miriam, as the only child – her mother was terrified of child-birth – was worshipped: hothoused, even. She lived in what she called a "fortress family". Her father, a shy, retiring man, had, as she put it, "married into an explosion and he didn't really know for the rest of his life how to deal with it." Her father, she explained, never wanted to be noticed. "My mother did, and I do. You know, I'm upset if people don't notice me, which is a bit pathetic actually but that's the truth!"

I wondered, though, whether there was a downside to this self-contained "fortress" family. Didn't her friends, for example, complain that she spent so much time with her family that they couldn't get to see her? Maybe, she retorted. "But I was never held back from friendship and one of the things I am proudest of in my life is the friends that I have made all over the world. I find it easy to make friends because I'm confident. My parents gave me confidence and so I can reach out to people unafraid, and I have wonderful friends.

"No, they never stopped me from making friends. They may have made it difficult for friends to come to my house but Mummy was very hospitable. Her tomato sandwiches were the talk of the town!"

And yet, I pressed her, wasn't there something unusually intense, maybe even unnaturally intense, about this passionate familial love? Miriam agreed that was true of her relationship with her mother. "I used to get into bed with Mummy every day, every single day until she died," she told me. "Or until I left home, anyway. And we would talk about the world and every-thing that we thought and people. We shared everything. She had a huge effect on me."

But despite, or perhaps because of, their closeness, it was Miriam's insistence on complete openness, on telling her mother everything, that led to one of the biggest regrets of her life. Because just three days after she had told her mother she was gay, her mother had a stroke. Surely, I suggested, she might have predicted this reaction – so why did she have to tell her?

"I can't hold back from anything," she replied. "I'm telling you everything. That's the way I was brought up, to be open . . . and therefore it was natural for me to talk to my mother about everything and I think that's right."

Nonetheless, she continues to blame herself for that stroke and for the awful aftermath of the stroke which meant that for seven years her mother continued to live in a wordless prison. A woman characterised by exuberance, noise, constant talking, was condemned to silence. And for those seven years Miriam looked after her.

"It is a catastrophe that felled her in a moment," she said. "And it was the worst time of my life." But when she died, I suggested, although it must have been very painful to lose such an adored parent, wasn't there a sense of liberation, too? Not just that her mother's suffering was over, but that Miriam herself was somehow now freed to get on with her life. Surely her mother wouldn't have been able to accept Miriam's partner, might have tried to break up that relationship?

"Yes, I believe she would," Miriam agreed. "Because she would've felt it was wrong. She felt homosexuality was an aberration, something not exactly disgusting, but pitiful. And she would not have accepted it in me. She simply would not have accepted it. And I don't agree with that. I think you're born or it comes upon you and you go with it. I'm who I am and that was the path I took and that's where I am and I defend it, even though, in a way, I don't have to defend that. But Mummy would not have accepted it."

Despite such disagreements, and despite the deep sadness Miriam Margolyes still feels at the loss of such a powerful figurehead, it's clear that this overwhelming, obsessive family love gave her the confidence, the panache, the strength and the principles that still inform her life and art.

A short time after I'd talked with her, she cropped up on one of those late-night chat shows where her presence can be guaranteed to provide not just some well-honed show-business anecdotes but also some amiable subversion of the genre itself. On this occasion she was joined on the sofa by the "famous" actor Dominic Cooper. Not only did she fail to recognise him but she also casually damned the film, *Mamma Mia*, in which he'd starred. "That was a dreadful film," she said.

It's this honesty, which might in other spheres attract some admiration, that has occasionally led to Miriam being categorised as at best "anarchic" and at worst "eccentric". The latter term is even more frequently levelled at another of the women celebrities whose childhood I was anxious to understand: the writer and TV presenter Lucinda Lambton.

When we first met, at a book launch held in a gloomy Pall Mall club, she was in something of a mild panic. It seemed that her car had been moved from where she'd parked it in the Mall and taken to an underground car pound some miles away. Would she like me to help her find the place? Although it took no more than half an hour to reunite Lucinda with her car, I was flattered to find that she now regarded me as a firm friend.

On other social occasions, at that early point in the evening when I was still nervously looking around for a familiar face, I'd find that she was suddenly and rather wonderfully standing in front of me, smiling and bursting with that contagious enthusiasm that has always informed her crusades on behalf of England's forgotten architectural heritage, as well as her scores of TV documentaries about neglected or under-appreciated buildings.

Her latest obsession, she told me as as our interview began, is "a terrific, terrific exciting book . . . it makes me feel faint to think about it." And the subject? "Buildings in the shape of elephants. And, my God, they're exciting! Napoleon commissioned a giant

12-storey-high elephant to stand in the Bastille built out of cannons of the vanquished Spanish: a bronze vast elephant painted in so many ways in beautiful water colours."

Erudite and unendingly inquisitive, Lucinda Lambton is astonishingly modest, insisting repeatedly that she has no education to speak of, no scholarly background. This, she explained, is because she always felt she was regarded at home as worthless, a bit of a nuisance.

Her relationship with her father, the now disgraced Lord Lambton, was particularly troubled. And it dominated her subsequent views of men, of life, of complexity. "I admired him more than liked him," she mused. Then she added, with characteristic self-deprecation, "He didn't like me either, which was difficult. He loved all his other children and I was . . . the explanation might be that I'd been the reason for him having to marry my mother, with whom he wasn't happy."

She had a spectacularly stormy relationship with her father, one coloured by almost Dickensian episodes of cruelty and anger. "A story comes to my mind of a great shooting lunch with all the people attired in their plus fours all the way down the table. And he read my diary out to the table when I was 14 or 15," she remembered. "And I threw a glass of water in his face and he came over and pulled my hair back and put his foot on my chest and poured a bottle of cherry brandy into my face with everybody cheering him. That sort of thing was bad."

Bad – but somehow formative, too. The spats with her father, she thought, became like a game. "I likened it to . . . what's it called – real tennis?" It was as though these two powerful personalities recognised something of themselves in each other. Not so much that Lucinda, in crude Freudian terms, was in love with her father, exactly. More that she identified with him. So, in another shocking way, he taught her to be herself.

But she'd be the first to admit that he wasn't exactly a good person. "He was seriously at fault for the bad things he did," she conceded. And the most public of these was his affair with a call girl – a disgrace that lost him his senior post in the Ministry of Defence. And for the press, the details of the affair were irresistible. Senior Tory Lord Lambton was pictured all over the papers in bed with a prostitute, pictures that had been snapped by the woman's husband, who'd been hiding in a cupboard.

Meanwhile, Lucinda was travelling across London with her two young sons, anxiously trying to shield them from the newspapers. "And everybody was holding up their paper so you saw the headlines, 'Lambton – Call Girl and I', 'Lambton – Call Girl and I' . . . And I didn't think it was the ideal moment to teach them the facts of life."

But though she might have been embarrassed, she was never shocked. In fact, she went and stayed with him "because there was nobody there". For, like all of my women guests who spoke to me about their parents, Lucinda Lambton was unendingly forgiving.

She was more than forgiving to her mother: she absolutely worshipped her, even though this was a mother who had very little time for her. The youngest of a family of daughters, Lucinda was sent away to boarding school at the age of eight.

And, she agreed, it was a lonely, desolate time. "I remember ringing home from a dark, cold and lonely linoleum-covered passageway. And the telephone being answered, and hearing the roar of a party. And you could hear all the laughter of the men and women, the music, the clinking drinks, the ice. This terrific roar, and then my mother would say, 'I'm sorry, I can't talk now, darling,' and put down the receiver."

As soon as Lucinda reached adolescence her mother said, "You've got bosoms and things. You can leave school now." This mother, she recalled, was infamous for having a raging affair with the artist Lucien Freud. And although she was rather neglectful, far too busy partying to have much time for her children, Lucinda adored her spirit, her gaiety.

Lucinda also acknowledged that she and her mother were rather similar. "We can talk the hind legs off a donkey with anyone all the time and she was very, very good at that. She was a crashing terrible snob and a liar," she told me, before adding somewhat sheepishly: "It was gratuitous and nasty of me to say that. She was also terrific."

Eventually her mother had a dreadful accident – go-karting. And after that came an even worse accident, a car crash on the A1 that left her unable to walk. But even that didn't crush her spirit. "She kept her pecker up, I never knew her complain once. And she was very, very ill all the time and in terrible pain but she never once complained."

It was that indomitable spirit that Lucinda Lambton so admired. "She was great," she insisted. "I miss her liveliness very much . . . She was so funny and so lively and so great." And, Lucinda remembered, she kept that lively spirit right up to the very last moment.

"She died singing 'Cocaine Bill and Morphine Sue'," Lucinda told me, "It was a drug-addict song. She died singing it in her bed. She was a lively woman."

Now in the graveyard on the hill
Lies the body of Cocaine Bill.
And in the grave right by his side
Lies the body of his cocaine bride.
All o' you cokies is a'gonna be dead
If you don't stop sniffin' that stuff in your head.

Chapter Ten

Who Needs Friends?

*Stephen Fry – Michael Winner – Uri Geller – Frank Oz – John Lydon
–Andre Previn*

**Harry Belafonte and E.L.Doctorow meet for the first time in the In
Confidence studio**

We knew that Dave was drinking too much. We knew that he was
always the first to suggest going round to the pub at the end of
the working day, just as we knew that he always finished his
drink before anyone else, was always eager for the next round,
was nearly always left behind in the bar when the rest of us
decided it was time for home. But although we talked to each
other about Dave's drinking, not one of us mentioned our
concern to Dave himself.

Part of the problem was his status. He'd been working at

Broadcasting House for longer than most of us and was univer-
sally regarded as a larger-than-life character. He wasn't just
Dave, he was "good old Dave". And everybody wanted him to
go on being "good old Dave". Only a spoilsport moralist would
want to suggest that he might cut down on the juice that fuelled
his exceptional sociability.

But after one particularly sad evening in The George when it
had become obvious to anyone who looked that Dave was now
drowning rather than waving, I decided to have a word with
Graham, the person in the group who seemed to be his closest
friend. Didn't he think it was time to have a word with Dave
about his drinking?

"Not really," said Graham.

"But aren't you his closest friend?"

"That's the whole point," said Graham, closing the conversation. "Friends are people you don't try to change."

It was a definition of friendship that often came back to me as
I watched some of the cocaine-fuelled antics at several well-
known private London clubs in the '80s. There was usually a
recognisable group: one or two celebrities, a clutch of lesser stars,
and three or four nonentities who were desperately eager to be
accepted as full participants.

Even from a distance it was easy to see that there would be
casualties amongst these extras. They might be able to prove
their membership of the set by drinking and smoking and
snorting along with the stars, but unlike them they didn't have a
car waiting outside the club to see them safely home. Neither did
they have a personal assistant or an agent to calm their anxieties
or boost their confidence, or indeed a job that paid enough to
support their nightly indulgences. When the star left the room,
these "friends" were exposed as nothing of the sort. For all their
earlier jokes and energetic banter they were now revealed, even
to the busy bar staff, as little more than sad hangers-on.

Social scientists who write about friendship like to talk about the time when social hierarchy dominated friendship patterns, a time when one's friends were almost invariably people who shared the same occupation, social class and geographical location. Nowadays, say such commentators, such rigid bonds have slackened and we are free to select our friends on the basis of mutual interest and emotional affinity.

This happy development, however, is hardly evident within a celebrity culture where the subtlest of differences in star status are every bit as constitutive of social relationships as the staircase at Downton Abbey. One doesn't have to spend time at the Oscars or the Cannes Film Festival to know that stars choose their friends from the same firmament as themselves.

But could this be more a matter of compulsion than choice? Those who enjoy true celebrity status do after all share similar problems and dilemmas. Getting together might make practical sense. Did Stephen Fry, for instance, feel that it was possible to have friends who did not in some respect share his celebrity status?

"Not all my friends are celebrities," he replied. "The friends I had from university are still my friends." But what gets in the way of those previous friendships, he admitted, is money. He's got so used to luxury. "I can't really see the point, with the money I have, of ever turning right when I get on to any aeroplane . . . And so if I'm going on holiday with friends, it's tricky because I don't want to travel differently, but I don't want to take a plunge in lifestyle and luxury just because I'm with them ."

And besides, he added, it's much easier to relax with people who share your lifestyle – famous people. "Certainly back in my Groucho days when there was a lot of, you know, playing snooker with the boys from Blur and Keith Allen and Damien Hirst and so on. We must have been rather forbidding for those who popped their heads up from another room and saw us all and thought, 'Oh, well they're a sort of clique.'"

And while Fry could see that the "clique" might be rather off-putting, it was for him a comfort zone. "Yes, it's true. One can relax in front of such people because you know who each other are, and each has as much to lose if we're behaving badly. So none of them is going to sneak to the newspapers because they'll be as likely to suffer from it as me."

But although Fry's honesty is refreshing, it leaves another important question about celebrity friendship unresolved. How many of those around him in the snooker room at the Groucho Club would qualify as real friends, if, for example, we used the definition of genuine friendship provided by Aristotle?

"It is those who desire the good of their friends for their friends' sake that are most truly friends, because each loves the other for what he is, and not for any incidental quality."

It was his readiness, almost his eagerness, to talk about his showbiz friends that made me so anxious to interview Michael Winner. From reading his newspaper columns I'd formed the impression of someone who had a very distinctive take on famous friends. Michael, who sadly died a short time after we'd talked, had, of course, first acquired fame as one of Britain's more successful film directors, the man responsible for dozens of rather modestly reviewed action movies as well as the hugely popular and, some would say, crudely populist *Death Wish* series. But his readiness to lampoon his enemies and his appetite for Jewish jokes in his regular *Sunday Times* column suggested a refreshing degree of cynicism about the whole notion of celebrity. He was notoriously critical, for example, of celebrity chefs.

"They're a joke, aren't they? A joke. A joke. Why are they celebrities? We'll have celebrity plumbers soon. And celebrity road-sweepers. They should shut up and stay in the kitchen. How a chef becomes a celebrity I do not know."

But this nicely jaundiced reflection on the spread of celebrity culture did not in any way imperil his love of those he regarded as proper stars, the stars of the silver screen. What's more, he believed that he had this special gift for developing real friendships with such people. All he had to do was work with them. Charles Bronson and Faye Dunaway and Robert Mitchum might all be notoriously difficult people but once Michael got to work with them on a film, there was no problem. They became friends. And that was that.

I told Michael that it all sounded a little too good to be true. Hadn't he also worked with Orson Welles? He hardly sounded or looked like a man who was in search of a new friend.

"Orson was adorable," Winner told me. "And a kind man. A damaged man. But he was also my friend. He said to me before our film started, 'You know, Michael, I write some of the lines, because, you know, I wrote the famous Ferris-wheel scene in *The Third Man*.' And I said, 'Orson, if you wrote that scene, you can rewrite anything because you're a genius, dear.' And after that we were friends."

It would be easy to dismiss Michael Winner's claims to enjoy so many friendships with the stars as nothing more than showbiz bragging. But even in this early part of our conversation, I was beginning to realise that what even such difficult stars as Mitchum and Welles found genuinely endearing about him was his reluctance or inability to do anything other than speak his mind. It was, I then learned, a quality that appealed to an even more notoriously difficult star.

"Marlon Brando was my dearest friend," he reminisced. "We spoke almost every day till the day he died. He was the most marvellous man."

Brando valued him, Winner told me, because he was a straight talker. "Marlon Brando said the most wonderful thing that's ever been said about me. He said, 'Michael Winner is the only person I've ever met who does not talk to me in the way he thinks I wish to be spoken to.'"

And Brando was not a man who found it easy to relax, or to

trust. "His make-up man who'd been with him for 30 years said, 'You're the only person he's behaved like this to. You got him laughing, you kept him laughing, you got him off balance and he adored you.' And in his autobiography he says that my film *The Nightcomers* was the only film he ever enjoyed making."

It was, I thought, an extraordinarily odd but also strangely credible friendship. There did seem to have been some real affection between these two different people: one of them affable, expansive, heart-on-sleeve, loquacious – the other moody, secretive, suspicious, sullen. What seemed to unite them apart from frankness was a nagging, ever-present sense of the absurdity, even the worthlessness, of fame. It was something captured by the two questions that, according to Winner, Brando regarded as the most important questions of all: "How happy have I been in life?" and "How much am I worth naked in the street?"

On the basis of this evidence, it would seem churlish to regard Michael Winner's assertions of friendships with the stars as little more than name-dropping. There was clearly some happy reciprocity involved in his many celebrity relationships. It would, however, be difficult to be equally generous about the range of friendships claimed by Uri Geller.

This self-confessed lover of publicity, whose claim to fame continues to rest almost entirely upon his capacity to bend household spoons, has a veritable cutlery set of friends. His website is peopled with celebrity associates: Clint Eastwood, John Lennon, Elton John. And we were hardly into our conversation before he was telling me about his affection for Salvador Dali and the intimacy he enjoyed with John Lennon and Elvis Presley.

But, I asked him, were any of these people real friends in the usual sense of the word or merely people who at some time or another had been impressed by his powers – powers that apparently for legal reasons he now prefers to describe as "mystifying" rather than as "psychic"? Did these people ring him for a chat? Come round for dinner and a drink?

"Many of them. I stay in touch. Of course I do. Some of them of course just took a picture and probably I'll never hear from them again because they're so huge as superstars living somewhere in Beverly Hills and they're busy with their movies. I came from a poor family, we had no money, and suddenly I became fantastically famous, suddenly I meet these unbelievable people like Elvis and John Lennon. And they mesmerised me. And decades ago in the '70s I was obsessed with fame and fortune. I wanted to be noticed. I wanted to be a super-psychic rock star. I wanted to imitate them. I wanted the limos. I wanted the private jets and yachts and I wanted to go to Cannes and Cap Ferrat. And that brought me down. Because when I had fame and fortune I became desperately sick because I just couldn't handle it. I became bulimic. I was killing myself. I was dying."

But as we continued to talk about friendship, I learned of a most surprising relationship which almost because of its sheer unlikeliness stood out from the smoother "Uri-Geller-on-demand" anecdotes. This relationship was with the one person whom Geller regarded not so much as a friend but as a "soul mate": Michael Jackson.

"I'm hugely controversial," he explained. "From the day I came out in Israel, I was attacked: left, right and centre. So I learned how to live with controversy. I knew how to use it. Michael was also hugely controversial. There was some kind of understanding between us of what he was going through and of what I was going through. He also believed in spirituality. He loved mind power. He loved stories of the universe and beyond. He loved Albert Einstein and Carl Jung. Michael was a phenomenon."

They met, he told me, over 15 years ago and "clicked". "Then he saw some of my drawings and wanted me to design his album.

And we had this amazing relationship." He paused then, his face darkened. "Until the devastating day when I introduced him to Martin Bashir. Which to this day I really feel guilty about."

He was referring to the TV interview in which Bashir asked Jackson questions about young boys, and the response was thought by commentators to be extremely compromising.

"Michael did some awesomely devastating mistakes in that interview. He sat there with a 13-year-old boy, holding his hand, telling the camera that it's okay to invite kids to his bed and put them to sleep with warm milk."

Notwithstanding these revelations, Uri Geller stood by his friend. "First of all I want to make this clear, that Michael was totally innocent, and, as we all know, he was found to be totally innocent in a court of law." And, not content even with that exoneration, Geller went on to attempt his own proof of innocence. He hypnotised Jackson, asked about his relations with young children and found no sign of guilt. His faith in Jackson had been confirmed by the faith he had in his own powers.

It was, I thought, too easy to dismiss this mutuality as a *folie à deux*. Uri Geller's love of his friend, and his loyalty to him in unpromising circumstances, seemed crazily genuine.

"The day Michael died," he told me, searching for the best words, "it was, it was utterly devastating."

For a moment at least I sensed that "Uri Geller" had left the stage.

There was another form of celebrity friendship that I hoped to explore. Even as a child I'd always wondered how some of the better-known double acts behaved together when they were no longer on stage or before the cameras. How well did Abbott get on with Costello? Were Laurel and Hardy close mates? What did Dean Martin really think about Jerry Lewis?

It was this sort of curiosity that made me particularly excited at the prospect of interviewing the puppeteer and film director Frank Oz, who I knew had endured an exceptionally long and very collaborative relationship with the creator of the *Muppets*, Jim Henson.

Henson, who died of a streptococcal infection back in 1990 when he was only in his early 50s, had picked up a wagonload of awards for his role in creating *Sesame Street* and *The Muppet Show*. But he had always gone out of his way to acknowledge the vital role played by Oz in all his achievements. How had they first come together?

Frank told me that as a teenager he'd been following in his parents' footsteps by producing a couple of minor puppet shows: nothing very fancy, just enough to make a little extra pocket money. But in the audience at one such show had been Jim Henson. Only a little later he offered young Frank a proper job.

"I was 19 and I had to move to New York. I've got to say my family should be taking the credit, my mother and father allowed a 19-year-old to go to New York by himself and live by himself in an apartment. I'm now the father of four adult kids, one of whom is 19. I can't imagine sending her to New York alone! It's scary! So they took a huge supportive chance but the only reason they did was they knew Jim, got very familiar with Jim, liked him a lot and trusted him."

Did he form an instant friendship with Jim Henson?

"Oh, no. I was 19, I was just a kid. I went to the studio in Second Avenue, New York; it was two rooms, that's all, just two rooms and a nook for a secretary. There were only four of us. And I was the junior member. So I wasn't at a particular place where I could have a relationship with Jim because I was working for Jim and everything was new and extraordinary. It was only later, after years and years and years of doing hundreds of shows, flying everywhere with him, driving with him, we became very very close like brothers and that's when I got to know him. But it took a while for that to happen."

And one of the qualities Oz admired most about Jim was his loyalty to those around him. He was supportive even when people weren't really up to his exacting standards.

"Many many people should've been fired. He was extraordinarily patient and always saw the good in people, always. He was a very singular human being. He cared about the quality of the work and if people really gave 120 per cent he was very patient with them and he wouldn't fire them. I'd say I'd treated Jim like a father in the beginning because I was 19, but I had no right to do that. He had kids of his own. I would be moody as a kid. But he was very very patient and he did not ever tell us what to do. Never. He never said, Do this. He just did what he did and we went with it and we learned that way."

And Jim was a perfectionist. Even when The Muppets were used for commercials, he would insist on the same high quality.

"We'd do things like the Cloverland Cow commercial or Wilson's Meats or whatever it was. Now some people might be cynical: I gotta make this money. But no matter what Jim did he had fun. He didn't say, 'Oh, Jeez, I gotta make this money.' He did the very best he could. He had a lot of fun doing it and worked like hell. We all learned from that."

So Jim's death hit Frank hard. It was almost like a father dying.

"Yeah, father, brother. We were very, very close. If he'd only gotten to hospital two hours earlier he would've been saved but this extraordinary vicious infection was too fast and it was a terrible week."

But of course Henson wasn't just a father-figure to Frank. He was also a close colleague. They worked together so closely on *The Muppets* that it must have been difficult to distinguish between their puppet characters and their real selves – especially when it came to the flirty, squabbling banter between Kermit and Miss Piggy. How much, I wondered, was that relationship really about them?

"Yeah, no question. When I created Piggy with the writers, I created a very neurotic character. She has layers of inner conflict, layers – and that was me. At that time I had tremendous inner conflict with many things, one of which was that I didn't want to be a puppeteer, I wanted to direct but I was too scared to say it to myself. Jim on the other hand always went with the flow, always. He didn't paddle upstream. He always went with it, went with it. And so that was our relationship in real life and that tended to be our relationship with the puppets also."

I did, of course, talk to Frank Oz about those other parts of his career that had not involved such close collaboration with Jim Henson: his work as director on such films as *Little Shop of Horrors*, and, of course, the fame he acquired later in life as the voice of Yoda in the *Star Wars* series of films. But, often without any prompting from me, the conversation would revert to his friendship with Jim. It occurred to me after the interview that the reason for the exceptional strength of their relationship had already been hinted at in Frank's account of the interaction between Miss Piggy and Kermit. Matters that could not be discussed face to face could readily be tackled through the medium of the puppets. In the roles of Miss Piggy and Kermit they could say what they liked to each other. They had an alibi to hand. It was the puppets who were doing the talking. Not them.

Frank Oz came to the studio with his new wife Victoria, who like other partners was able to watch the interview being filmed. This was not, however, always a completely harmonious arrangement. During my interview with the distinguished barrister Michael Mansfield, for example, his wife Yvette leaned forward on a couple of occasions and fretted that no one in the studio had persuaded him to do up his jacket properly. "Why *does* he look like that?" she asked rhetorically. "Why?"

Howard Jacobson's wife Jenny, on the other hand, had no complaints about her husband's appearance but showed concern when he began to sit forward in his interview seat as the conversation turned to Howard's views on Israel. "Oh, no, don't do that," she whispered. "He always does that when he's worried."

But perhaps the most significant matrimonial intervention came from Harry Belafonte's wife Pamela. Upon learning that later in the day I was to be interviewing the award-winning novelist E. L. Doctorow, she suddenly revealed that, although Doctorow was her father's closest friend, Harry and Doctorow had never met face to face. It was an intervention that subsequently allowed me to introduce Harry Belafonte, a man who had been present at several of the most critical moments in American political history and had met many of the great players in the civil rights movement, to the foremost chronicler and reinterpreter of American legends, E. L. Doctorow.

But such momentous interventions from spouses were rare. Most of my 60 guests arrived at the studio in the company of minders of various sorts: personal assistants, publishing representatives, even, in one case, a personal make-up lady. Only one of these ever made any real impression. This was John Lydon's minder, manager, hairdresser and lifelong friend John Rambo. This, I quickly learned, was far from being an ordinary celebrity–minder relationship. Rambo was a tough-talking no-nonsense representative of the values that were so cherished by Lydon himself.

"I've known Johnny Rambo for 40 years," he told me. "I think of all the managers I've had and been through, all of them critically acclaimed and every one of them a ferret, a rat and a cheat and a fraud and a liar for various reasons, and the only person that I can trust is someone who would be viewed as working-class scum, illiterate Mr Rambo Stevens, a man who won't lie to me, won't cheat me, and I won't lie or cheat to him."

It was a friendship, he told me, based on values. "I think our values are better than any values I've seen from any of the so-called well-educated managers that are floating around out there. And John had to, like me, learn the hard way what management meant. I mean, John came to work with me first originally with the Pistols as our private – our personal security . . ."

It was John Rambo who stood by him when he started his current band, PIL, and John Rambo who arranged for Lydon to take on the butter commercial that brought him such criticism. Wasn't it true, I suggested, that by doing a butter advertisement he was selling out?

Not at all, he replied. It was the revenue from that commercial that allowed him to start up PIL, and it was John – or Rambo – who had the imagination to see that. "Sold out what?" he scoffed. "You'll not get John to drop his values. That's not possible."

Lydon and Rambo were in so many ways a powerful and very touching example of how a real Aristotelian friendship could be maintained in the jealous, status-shifting world of celebrity. One only had to think of some of the crises Lydon had endured over the years to realise the strains that must have been placed on their togetherness: the controversial times with Malcolm McClaren, the tragic death of Lydon's stepdaughter Ari Up (the lead singer in the punk band The Slits), Lydon's alleged involvement in several well-reported physical assaults, his angry departure from *I'm a Celebrity . . . Get Me Out of Here!*

But although I was moved by this friendship, it was in a way somewhat less strange than the relationship I discovered when I talked with Andre Previn.

During my conversation with the celebrated composer and conductor I'd been constantly amazed at the sheer range of his contacts in the worlds of film and jazz and classical music. He seemed to have worked and been good friends with everybody from film and stage director Vincente Minnelli to composer and conductor Leonard Bernstein. And then there were the wives: night-club singer Betty Bennett, singer-songwriter Dory Previn (née Langdon), actress Mia Farrow, diplomat's daughter Heather Sneddon and classical violinist Anne-Sophie Mutter. Did they count as friends as well? Oh, yes. "Of course. We are the best of friends. There is no acrimony between us. I'm a lucky man."

I tried another tack. Was there anyone he didn't know? How about Sam Goldwyn? Did they meet during the '40s and '50s when Andre was busy composing and transcribing film scores? Oh, yes. Of course.

"I remember sitting in his office together with the director Reuben Mamoulian, who asked Sam what he was planning to give his wife for her birthday. And Goldwyn said, 'Well,' he said, 'you know, Frances has beautiful hands, so I'm having a bust made of them.'"

But of all the personalities who'd peopled Previn's long and colourful life, there was one he regarded as a true friend, a really true friend. And who was that? Previn gave me his name as though he was mentioning an amiable pal or a sociable neighbour rather than the most controversial comedian in American entertainment history.

"Lenny Bruce and I were friends. We appeared in the same club in San Francisco and we took a walk once past a bookshop called Books Incorporated on Sutter Street. And they had the new three-volume edition of the Mozart letters translated by Emily Anderson, and they were 25 dollars. Well, this is a long time ago and 25 dollars might as well have been a thousand. I didn't have it. And I mentioned that to Lenny, who was with me, and we went to a coffeehouse and sat down and ordered coffee, and Lenny said, 'I'll be right back.' And he left. He came back about ten minutes later with his voluminous coat, and he opened the coat and there were the three volumes.

"He said, 'Here, I stole these for you.' I said, 'Lenny, what?' And he said, 'I stole them for you.' And he put them down. He said, 'Here, a present.' And I said, 'Lenny, you can't do that. I can't take that. I mean – you were a thief, you can't do that.' And he got angry, he got seriously angry. He said, 'Look, if I had 25 dollars to give you as a present, that is not a big present, because I could have said, Here you are and bought the books. But,' he said, 'I violated my parole with this.' And he said, 'It's a big present, man, because if I get caught I go back to the slammer.'"

So Andre Previn graciously accepted the stolen goods. "I said, 'Well, okay, Lenny, it's very sweet of you. Sign the books then.' And he took Volume One and he wrote 25 dollars, crossed it out, put 15, crossed it out, 10, crossed it out, and when he got down to a dollar, he crossed it out and he wrote under it, 'Take it, schmuck, nobody's looking.' And signed his name. Well, I bet I can safely say that I'm the only man who has the collected letters by Mozart signed by Lenny Bruce."

Part Four

Identity

Chapter Eleven

Women's Studies

Ann Leslie – Sheila Hancock – Joan Bakewell – Fay Weldon

It was early in the '80s and I was taking a seminar on Max Weber's account of the role of the Protestant Ethic in the development of capitalism when the phone on my desk began to ring. I asked the semi-circle of first years to excuse me while I took the call.

"Laurie Taylor?" queried a carefully articulated male voice.

"That's me."

"My name is Michael Ember and I'm ringing from BBC Radio 4. Would you mind if I asked you a question?"

At that time in my life, calls from the media were not that rare. I'd somehow allowed myself to drift into the role of media sociology don, turning up on the front row of daytime discussion programmes to deliver opinions on everything from teenage drug-taking to mid-life crisis. It was a rather unworthy desire to be in the media spotlight, which *Private Eye* once characterised as "sounding off one's mouth at the drop of a cheque".

However, on this occasion, my caller seemed unaware of my specialist concerns.

"May I ask your views on the recent increase in the cost of a postage stamp?"

"Well," I stuttered, holding up an apologetic hand to the seminar group, "it could be very good news for those who are only too pleased to dispense with the old-fashioned formality of a letter and would prefer the much greater immediate reciprocity provided by a phone call."

"Thank you," said the voice. "But what would you say against the increase? What might be the bad effects?"

"I suppose," I mused, a trifle wearily, "one could regret that the careful delineation of opinion and emotion in a written letter is now going to be replaced by the phatic form of communication – the 'um's and 'er's and 'you know's that constitute the bulk of most telephone conversations."

"Very good," said Mr Ember. "Are you free to take part in a programme called *Stop the Week* on Friday of this week?"

That was the beginning of an involvement that lasted for the best part of 20 years, allowing me to develop passing friendships with many of the other participants, among them chairman Robert Robinson and regular guests Milton Shulman, Anthony Clare, Nicholas Tucker and Michael O'Donnell.

But not one of these relationships proved quite as long-lasting or as deep as that which I developed over the years with the programme's most regular female guest: Ann Leslie.

Our first meetings, though, were hardly auspicious. Not only did Ann work for the *Daily Mail*, that bastion of alarmist conservatism, but she was also liable to turn up on any programme where the producer needed a woman to pour scorn upon a radical feminist perspective.

As if this was not already enough to raise my hackles, I also discovered when we met face-to-face that she dressed in a manner that flew in the face of all the articles I'd read about the need for modern liberated women to resist masculine attempts to turn them into "glamour objects". Ann didn't so much ignore these feminist injunctions as flout them: she wore bright primary-coloured outfits, extravagant amounts of make-up, lurid lipstick, tons of mascara and the most ostentatiously false eyelashes I'd ever seen.

It took me some time to realise that she thoroughly relished the effect her opinions and appearance were having on me. What could be more fun than to taunt a politically correct leftie sociologist from a provincial university?

But, as I increasingly recognised the game she was playing

and learned to laugh along with her jibes about my political seriousness, I also came to realise that Ann was truly more of an anarchist than a conservative. I also discovered, when I began to read her extensively researched and finely written *Daily Mail* reports from war zones around the world, that she was a formidable foreign correspondent, an eye-witness to many of the most significant events in the past 50 years and someone thoroughly deserving her clutch of British Press Awards.

I began our interview by asking a question that I'd never dared put to her even during the heavy drinking sessions that invariably followed a recording of *Stop the Week*. How much of her appearance, I asked, was just an act? I reminded her that although she had been made a Dame in 2006 for her "services to journalism", one commentator had observed that the award was redundant. Ann, he wrote, had always been a Dame.

"That's probably because I give that impression. I'm actually a wee timorous beastie at heart. I have to psyche myself up to look as if I'm in command. And actually that is partly why I became quite good at being a foreign correspondent, because round the world people are quite intimidated if they meet a woman who seems to be fearless. Even when I was a rather sexy young thing I could always inspire a bit of fear. Other women could use legs and bosoms. I used my ability to slightly alarm people."

But wasn't there a danger that her appearance might also deter people? Might not some find all her make-up and false eyelashes and glitter not so much aristocratic as, well, vulgar?

"That's funny. I think I am an Essex girl in some ways but I'm not in others. I just enjoy overdoing it. My daughter once said to me when she was a teenager and being as all teenagers are, disapproving of their parents, she said to me as I was setting sail for some social event with the full bling – the eyelashes, the lot – she said, 'Oh, Mummy, why do you have to be so Hendon?'"

How much did gender come into it? Was her appearance also part of the way of coping with the difficulties of being a female foreign correspondent in a very male world?

She didn't recognise the problem. "I'm often asked if it's terribly difficult being a woman in the mad, bad, macho parts of the world. And I say, 'No. It's absolutely fantastic being a woman.'" She referred me to the famous adventuress Freya Stark, who, in her book *Valley of the Assassins*, had got it spot on. Freya had noted that "the great advantage of being a woman is that everyone assumes you are much stupider than you are".

"And by 'everybody'," added Ann, "she meant men. Because they're completely fooled. I can play lots of roles with them. I can play either Daughter of the Raj" –Ann was born in India – "or Lady Bracknell, or a ditsy young girl."

She'd also added a new role to her repertoire: a dotty old woman.

"Dotty old women are ideal. First they exasperate a lot of those hardboiled ghastly war criminals because I remind them of their mothers. They also think dotty old women are completely harmless. That's fine. I love it. I love to switch. In one day in Israel and Palestine I remember switching from Daughter of the Raj to Lady Bracknell to dotty old woman. Worked perfectly. And men can't do that, can they? So I feel sorry for them."

This readiness to talk about the advantages women enjoyed in the world reminded me of the time, early in our relationship, when I'd plucked up enough courage to ask Ann why someone of her intelligence (I was quite capable at the time of using such a patronising phrase) was associated with reactionary politics. How and why had she become such a token right-wing anti-feminist? Her answer was brief. "There was," she told me, "a vacancy."

Did this mean she might be more sympathetic to feminists than she sometimes appeared on *Newsnight*? "I just got irritated with them because, of course, in a sense I was feminist. I'd no intention of being paid less than any man for doing the same job. I was feminist because I couldn't stand the way I was the highest paid columnist in Fleet Street in the '60s, and I wanted a mortgage. Ha, could I get one? No! So I was against the way we were discriminated against but feminism, you know, rushed off into a cul-de-sac. I remember being asked to a speculum party! I hope you don't know what that is." I shook my head nervously."This is where a group of feminists sit round in what they called a sacred circle or something like that. And because we're all ashamed of our bodies, we must embrace our bodies, we must recognise them. So the way you do that, you sit there with a speculum and peer up your innards and say, 'Oh, you are beautiful, my vagina!' and all this crap. You know, that's where it spun off into a mad cult."

It wasn't only the excesses of feminism that aroused Ann's sense of ridicule. She was equally scathing about celebrity culture. In her early days as a reporter she'd written a celebrity column and interviewed a huge range of stars: Ingrid Bergman, Tennessee Williams, Marlene Dietrich, David Niven, and James Mason (with whom she had an affair). It became very boring. The stars were "so over-interviewed, so over-rehearsed. I thought I'd rather interview countries." She didn't even want to talk about any of them. Marlon Brando was nothing but "a rude mumbling narcissist".

James Mason?

"Well," she allowed, "he was very clever and very sexy." She remembered that she'd described his voice as "sounding like soft footfalls in the dark". It was now "quite embarrassing".

But when I pressed her again on the subject of celebrity, she recalled an evening she'd spent with Dusty Springfield, a story that had all the condensed force of a parable.

"Poor Dusty. She was fantastic as a singer but she was a very lonely frightened person. I gave her a lift one evening because it was dusk. And I was driving along and she was looking out of the window. And I realised after a while that she was crying. It looked like it. It sounded like it. And she suddenly said, 'You know, I look through all these house windows in the evening because you can see into the kitchens and living rooms. You can see all these people enjoying a family life. And I feel so envious.' Because, of course, she didn't have any of this and she was never going to have it. She knew she was gay but she could never say it because it would have killed her in the musical world. So she took to drink, of course, and finally died. I was so sad for her because I knew she had this huge undertone of grief, because she could never replicate for herself what she could see at twilight through the windows of those houses."

It was, as I quickly realised from the start of the programmes, difficult to talk to female celebrities without mentioning gender politics. Newspapers and magazines that were ever eager to discuss such contemporary issues as working women, sexual permissiveness, abortion, marital infidelity, domestic violence, lesbianism and female objectification naturally sought out female celebrities whose lives and lifestyles provided telling personal illustrations of such issues and dilemmas.

Probably no celebrity ticked so many of these boxes as the actor and author Sheila Hancock. Although she can now boast a CBE and a well-deserved Lifetime Achievement Award from the 2010 Women in Film and Television Awards, she has had a life filled with personal setbacks and major tragedies.

She earned a scholarship to RADA but that was hardly the start of her intended career in acting.

"Back then it was a finishing school. It really was. There was the Honourable This and the Lady That, and they were going there to learn how to move and speak nicely and all that. So there was I, a working-class girl with a really bad London accent, amongst all these frightfully posh people. I was completely out of my depth and I hated it."

You said once that the only thing you learned there was that you had good legs?"

"Yes, there were some older boys at RADA, mainly ex-servicemen, and they used to make judgements on the girls and I remember being told that I had the best legs from the thighs down. So I felt quite good about my legs after that."

But this sort of self-regard was now a thing of the past.

"Well, I suppose it's partly because I'm an actress and have spent a lifetime looking at myself in the mirror, making up and all that, so I'm now actually bored. I know my face inside out. I know the bits that I have to hide. And I'm bored with the sound of my own voice. I'm often asked for opinions on things and if I ever hear it back, I think, 'Oh, God, there she goes again.'"

And the one subject on which her opinions were often sought was how on earth she managed to reconcile her much-advertised feminist opinions with her seemingly repetitive relationships with abusive men. Her father had been an alcoholic and her husbands Alec Ross and John Thaw, who both died tragically early, had been heavy drinkers. And yet she refused to accept that she had ever been a victim.

"I have seen personally, and certainly in the world at large, the huge damage that drink is doing," she allowed. "But there's no doubt that the men in my life had the volatility that came from the drinking very often and I must be drawn to that. Otherwise why would I continuously have done it, you know? So there is a part of me that likes the drama of that."

What did she mean by "drama"?

"I'm not good at contentment. I'm really not. I like excitement. I guess that's why I've twice been married to quite tempestuous men. I like not knowing what is going to happen next. Having men that are not predictable. Having men that will be absolutely wonderful one minute and then vile the next. I always feel I can deal with it. I'm streetwise so I think I'll be all right. I like not knowing what's round the corners. I wouldn't be in this profession if I didn't because you can't expect any continuity if you become an actor. You work from job to job."

It's not surprising perhaps that some feminists found this account hard to take. But some were even more outraged when it became publicly known that John Thaw had left her, for a time, when she was diagnosed with breast cancer. Then she was castigated for being even weaker, even more of a victim. She, however, seemed curiously understanding. "You don't have to be able to deal with other people's illnesses," she told me. "Some people really, really can't deal with it and they're made to feel guilty. Not everybody is able to nurture and care and be wonderful. They – they do it in other ways, you know. And John was so terrified that I was going to die. He was absolutely terrified and he couldn't deal with it. And I totally understood that."

Although I found Sheila's defence of John Thaw's behaviour extraordinarily generous, I could still admire her refusal to be predictable, her stolid unreadiness to denounce John for either his drinking or what others would see as his extreme callousness. It was perhaps paradoxical that of all my female guests it was Sheila who had the best feminist credentials. Not only had she spent time camping at Greenham Common, but she'd also had a passionate enthusiasm for the book that put her on the right path: Germaine Greer's *The Female Eunuch*.

"Oh, that book totally changed my life. Up until then without realising it I had thought that women were absolutely not as important as men. That we were there to look after men. In my day if you had an appointment to see a girlfriend, and then a boy asked you out, it was understood that you phoned your girlfriend and said, 'Oh, Tony's asked me out, I won't be coming.'

"Now, you know, you wouldn't do that, you wouldn't let your girlfriend down. I was in a play at the Royal Court and I was so amazed by this book that I got the other women in the company to read it and it flabbergasted all of us. So we formed a thing called The Group where we used to sit and talk about this revolutionary thinking. We used to meet up every Christmas and sit in the Peter Jones café opposite the Royal Court and raise a toast."

She told me that the Group still kept going even though one of its members had recently died. So at the last meeting, "there were just three of us in the photo we took at the table and then we started laughing and shrieking with laughter and the waiter came across and said, 'What are you laughing at?' And we said, we were wondering which one of us was going to be left to be in the next photo."

It wasn't Germaine Greer but Betty Friedan and her earlier work *The Feminine Mystique* that made the difference to journalist, TV presenter and Labour Party peer Joan Bakewell. Friedan's chronicle of the sad lives of suburban housewives did much to put the skids under the idea that a woman's proper place, the only place where she could be truly happy, was inside the home. That spoke directly to Joan.

"I'm part of that generation which moved on from the '50s when women were attracted to a man, married him, had children and stayed at home. And therefore weren't noticed very much at all. I was in a world where women were breaking out of that."

But for Bakewell this was far from being a complete liberation.

"I had arrived in the mid-'60s, before the feminist movement really got going. And I was in what was called a man's world. I was on a programme [*Late Night Line-up*] in which I was a woman presenter among three men.

"There were women: secretaries of course were all women. And some women producers. So it wasn't as though women were absent in the BBC, but I was the conspicuous one because I was on the screen. And therefore I got a lot of the girlie attention that went with that in the papers. I have to say I probably responded to it. It was very flattering and I liked being flattered."

But the pleasure she obtained from this "girlie attention" was, as she recognised at the time, difficult to reconcile with her newfound commitment to feminism.

"I went along to feminist meetings and on one occasion was denounced as having sold out."

How was she denounced?

"Someone came up to me in the course of all the arguing that was going on, I mean, I think she had dungarees and no make-up, that was a very important branch of feminism in those days, that you must reject make-up, attraction of any kind. And she came up and said to me, 'What are you doing here? You don't belong in this world, you belong in the man's world out there, you're showing off on television, you're – you're being called The Thinking Man's Crumpet.' And I was aghast and I said, 'But I want to see real change, can't you understand that? I mean, I really know the dilemmas that women have.' But whether I wanted to be flirty and pretty and admired, or whether I wanted to be a hard-nosed journalist and disregard my looks, I think I've probably tried to have the best of both worlds."

I had one last question for Joan.

"When I look back over your career," I said, "I can't help seeing a lack of parallel between your own career and the career of some of the men who were around at the same time as you during those early days. I'm thinking of people like Melvin Bragg or Alan Yentob or David Attenborough or Jonathan Miller. To an extent they have been able to have almost a progressive career, whereas your career has seemed to owe something to – a bit to accident, a bit to chance, a bit to something cropping up rather than you being completely recognised from your days on *Late Night Line-up*."

"Absolutely," she agreed. "When people say, 'Have you any regrets?' I always say that I regret that I never had such a career. I think I have to take the blame for myself in that I didn't recognise how steely and resolute I needed to be in a directional career. I was – I was taking pleasure in doing different things that I was offered, and I was reactive rather than proactive. I think it's also to do with my own character, a certain reticence, not shyness but a certain waiting for the world to happen to me instead of seizing it and driving it forward. And how broadcasting was then. I mean, men got the chances, there's no doubt about that, it's quite clear. And it's different now."

"Do you think perhaps you weren't angry enough?" I suggested. "You weren't perhaps passionate enough? Because when I read you, you do seem to have a sort of geniality, a sort of optimism that pervades quite a lot of your writing. And occasionally I think you are being a little bit – perhaps a little bit bland. A little bit taking things for granted rather than fighting them?"

She shifted in her seat. "Yes, I think that could be –" She hesitated. "That word 'bland' hurts."

"It's a nasty word."

"No, not only that, but Bland is my mother's maiden name. It's interesting."

"I remembered."

It was, perhaps, not too surprising to learn about the powerful influence of Germaine Greer and Betty Friedan upon my guests. When I was teaching sociology at York in the '80s, there were constant debates among academic staff and students about their preferred feminist texts. Should everyone be reading Friedan and Greer? Or should they take a more historical perspective and study Mary Wollstonecraft and Simone de Beauvoir? Or perhaps they should be more avant-garde and study Luce Irigaray and Judith Butler?

This debate also extended to fiction. Alice Walker and Sylvia Plath and Virginia Woolf and Doris Lessing were favoured authors. As was my guest Fay Weldon.

I'd first met Fay back in the late '80s when we'd both served on the Video Appeals Committee, a small body that was set up to hear appeals from film producers who felt that their particular video had been given an unnecessarily harsh certificate by the British Board of Film Classification.

Timothy Anderson

Fay Weldon: "In all my lies there's an element of truth."

The work mostly involved watching extremely innocuous sex movies (no actual sex, no visible genitalia and certainly nothing resembling an orgasm) and deciding whether they were fit to be sold or hired through normal retail outlets or were only to be marketed through licensed sex shops.

In my early days on the committee, I felt some trepidation about declaring an opinion in front of Fay. For although the videos were innocuous enough, they did almost invariably feature muscular men (often accompanied by a plumber's wrench) having their albeit simulated way with gaggles of enormously eager and grateful women.

So when we came to give our opinion on a video called *Sex Dens of Bangkok* (I'd originally read the title as *Sex Dons of Bangkok* and been foolishly looking forward to seeing an orgy of professors) I decided to wait until after Fay had delivered her judgement.

"It seemed somewhat salacious to me," said the chairman. "Perhaps best suited to the sex shops. Ms Weldon. What's your opinion?"

Fay gave the chairman one of her beguiling cat-uncoiling smiles before delivering her verdict. "Well," she said, "don't tell the sisters, will you, but it seems rather good. And all those girls. Well, they do seem to be enjoying themselves, don't they?"

It was not easy to tell whether this was her true opinion or whether she was simply being mischievous, confounding the committee chairman's expectations about how such a renowned feminist would respond to this bit of modest smut.

This mischievousness, or, as some would have it, perversity, had a wider effect when it became evident in her fiction. When she published her first novels, *The Fat Woman's Joke, Down Among the Women* and *Female Friends*, she was instantly hailed as a champion of women's rights and a chronicler of their struggle. Now, 35 novels later, she's aroused resentment and suspicion for seeming to turn her back on her earlier trenchant feminism. What explained this apparent inconsistency?

"The world is totally different now," she told me. "Society has changed totally in the last 40, 50 years. Gender relationships, if you're going to call them that, have changed totally. Women earn. Women make the life choices now that they used not to be able to do, therefore they're responsible for their actions and they can't go on blaming men for ever."

I reminded her of the battles she herself had had to fight in order to work in glamorous worlds like television, while also bringing up children. And yet now she seemed to be saying that women are better off staying at home and looking after their kids.

"You can't go on fighting on an old battleground where the battle has moved on," she reflected. "There are now all kinds of problems for women, brought on not by feminist ideas so much as by the capitalist world making, turning, obliging women to go into the labour force now when really they're trying to bring up their children, when they would be happier bringing up their children."

She paused and then added: "I think women used to be happier on their deathbeds or at least more contented than they are now."

"Look," I said, "we never really know where we are with you. You make all these statements but then you also say elsewhere that you might be lying or you claim that you only tell the truth when you are abroad because when you're there no one at home can read it. You've even confessed to having forged letters in your American literary archive."

Fay was a calm as ever.

"I'm a fiction writer, Laurie. I make things up. That's what I do, I'm sorry!"

But hadn't she also claimed that life was a fiction? Surely there must be some certainty somewhere?

"Well, the problem is that the truth changes. There's someone called a garbologist who goes through people's rubbish bins and works out how many tins of baked beans they've eaten even though they might say they haven't had any. You need to be a garbologist in your own life to know what really happened. You can't think the same thing every day, every morning."

There was only a little time left and I wanted to get away from lies and truth for a moment to ask Fay about her amazing productivity.

"You keep writing. So many novels. So many books that it's almost impossible to keep count. You've compared yourself to Sisyphus. Continually involved in hard work but really rather enjoying it. Endless pushing!"

"Yes, endlessly pushing, pushing this thing uphill which keeps falling down."

"You still enjoy writing? You write at speed, don't you? I read somewhere that it's like automatic writing. Or is that another lie?"

"Look, Laurie. In all my lies there's an element of truth. And that is probably the most important thing about them."

Chapter Twelve

Jew or Jew-ish?

Jonathan Miller – Frederic Raphael – Howard Jacobson –
Miriam Margolyes – Jackie Mason

My gentle Roman Catholic mother took every opportunity that came her way to undermine my father's intemperate atheism. She would recount an act of kindness she had observed while out shopping on South Road, and then, after she had drawn a modicum of attention from my father, would announce that the person who had enacted the kindness was a Catholic. "I've often seen her at St Helen's on a Sunday morning."

This might extract the occasional grudging nod from my father but even from an early age I think I always doubted whether someone whose commitment to atheism was only matched by his devotion to scientific method would be greatly impressed by these individual instances of Catholic altruism.

But my mother had another and more powerful proselytising weapon to hand: a 1950s celebrity singer. For reasons that were never quite clear, my father became inordinately fond of a song called "Galway Bay". He hummed it in the kitchen, sang a few lines as he went up and down stairs, and could manage an entire verse in the relative privacy of his garden shed.

My mother quickly realised that the song, apart from hymning the glories of sunsets over the eponymous bay, also contained a verse in which the singer explicitly referred to the likelihood of life after death. Had Dad realised what he was singing? Did he know the song was about the existence of eternity?

Father was unimpressed. A song was a song was a song. But then one day, after some extensive biographical trawling, mother came up with her trump card. The person who'd had such a big hit with his recording of "Galway Bay" was none other than Josef Locke, and Josef Locke, she'd heard, was not only a Catholic, but – wait for this – had once been seen by my mother's best friend, Mrs Duck, sitting in a pew at St Helen's church.

I fancy my father must have wilted a little under this fusillade because, as soon as a TV set arrived in our front room, my mother seized her chance for further assertions of the critical part played by Catholics in the celebrity culture of the day. "She's a Catholic," she would announce whenever Sophia Loren or Carmen Miranda made the briefest of appearances on the screen. Even the young children got in on the act. "He's a Catholic," my little brother would scream at Cliff Richard or Adam Faith. If Mother ever contradicted him, he'd have recourse to one of her own favourite ways of getting off the hook. "Well, he looks like a Catholic. He *looks* Catholic!"

I remembered this childhood way of distinguishing between TV stars when I was planning my interviews for Sky Arts. There was clearly no reason for believing, as my mother had, that subscription to a single religion was a useful way of making distinctions between celebrities.

There was, however, one cultural and religious affiliation that did seem to make a real difference to the manner in which my some of my interviewees viewed their own life and success: their Jewishness.

I doubt if Josef Locke was regularly regarded as a Vatican ambassador by members of his audience, but every one of my Jewish interviewees had at one time or another been called upon to explain the relevance of their affiliation to their life and their work.

Consider Jonathan Miller. I'd been a devoted fan since I'd first seen him in the original production of *Beyond the Fringe*. After that I used to look out for his every appearance on radio and television. I particularly relished his confident, unapologetic atheism.

"Did you hear what Jonathan Miller said about atheism on the *Today* programme this morning?" I'd ask my colleagues in the senior common room at York University. "He said he had no wish to describe himself as an atheist because why should there be a special word for someone who doesn't believe in God? After all, there's no special word for someone who doesn't believe in fairies. Isn't that good?"

But as I suspected before our interview began, none of these assertions of his lack of faith had fully allowed him to escape his Jewishness. He had, of course, already entered several books of quotations with his declaration in *Beyond the Fringe* that he was "not really a Jew. Just Jew-ish. Not the whole hog."

That, though, certainly hadn't been enough to deflect questions about his beliefs. There had been interviews in which he'd had to insist that he had no wish "to join the Jews" or any desire to engage in some form of "hypothetical solidarity" based on his Jewishness. He had on one occasion been ready to admit, albeit with some reluctance, that he had felt "a twinge of affinity with Jews in New York", but quickly ascribed such a feeling to their intellect rather than their Jewishness. New York Jews were clever. That was what made them interesting. Not their belief system.

So I decided to pursue his Jewishness from a slightly different angle. Now that he was older, I asked, did he have any regrets about his past life? Were there things that he wished he had done? Paths in the wood he might have taken?

"That's a question that I ask myself all the time. Ought I ever to have given up medicine?"

This wasn't, as he explained, a question prompted by a high-minded belief that a life in medicine would have enabled him to be of benefit to others.

"I was never interested in helping people," he explained. "I was not philanthropic in my medical interests. I was driven entirely, as I always have been about everything in my life, by a rapacious curiosity. I want to know how things work. And if I could have gone on doing what in fact was not really even named at that time, which was neuropsychology, I think I could have rendered a more valuable service than the one I've offered."

I reminded Jonathan that this was not the first time he'd expressed these regrets. Why should someone who'd had such a very distinguished career as a writer, broadcaster and theatre and opera director fret about the value of their life? Might this not be evidence of a Jewish sense of guilt, a feeling, even in the face of such considerable success, that things had not turned out as well as they might? What was that joke about the Jewish telegram? "Start worrying. Details follow."

Jonathan would have none of it. Although his own father had been a committed Jew, someone who "knew the scripts off by heart" and always warned his son that he would regret his lack of belief one day, he himself had no emotional or intellectual interest in the religion or the culture. He was adamant about that.

"Jewishness means nothing to me," he insisted as though wishing to move to another subject. I persisted. But surely there were moments when it became salient? I reminded him of a scene in a Frederic Raphael play in which a number of characters sitting at a dinner table began to exchange seriously anti-Semitic remarks. Would he have just sat there quietly while this went on around him?

This had more of an effect. Yes, he agreed, if Jewishness mattered so much to other people in his company then he would play his identity card. Indeed, it was only in the face of anti-Semitism that he ever became a Jew. "I'm a Jew for anti-Semites. But that's all."

But even this concession seemed too much for him. "Although I'm not offended as a Jew by anti-Semitic remarks. Anti-Semitic remarks offend my humanity."

Miller's modest concession reminded me of Jean-Paul Sartre's essay *Anti-Semite and Jew*, which he published shortly after the liberation of Paris from German occupation in 1944. In this essay, Sartre proposed that anti-Semitism played a key role in Jewish identity. Faced by such hostility, some Jews would embrace and even exaggerate their Jewishness. In contemporary terms they would "come out" as Jews, as "authentic Jews". Others would, in Sartre's terms, become "inauthentic" by choosing to efface their identity through assimilation. Both the authentic Jew and the inauthentic Jew, in Sartre's view, live wholly in the present – or at least that's how they're regarded by the anti-Semite, who dwells in a wholly fantasised past where no foreigners can intrude. By placing the Jews firmly in the here and now, the anti-Semite strips them of a past, a past where they belonged.

That air-brushing of the Jews from the imagined past is a theme that was elaborated by another of my guests, Frederic Raphael, the author of over 20 novels, including the televised *Glittering Prizes*, and the Oscar-winning screenplay of the 1965 hit film *Darling*. In his book *The Necessity of Anti-Semitism* he captures the manner in which the English compensate for their loss of Empire by constructing a fictional (and Jew-free) past. Was he talking about the fictions of nostalgia?

"Nostalgia is not really about longing for or dreaming about the past. It's actually about aching for home. I think the English suffer particularly from this because they feel as if it was a great period in their lives. But at the same time, of course, their writers spend an enormous amount of time pointing out that it wasn't really a great period at all. They point out that black people and natives of all kinds were ill-used, that the lower classes suffered terribly. And yet people keep thinking: 'I know, but it *was* wonderful, wasn't it, and why don't we go to Downton Abbey and live there?' And of course there are no Jews in *Downton Abbey* as there are no Jews in any part of that imagined golden age."

Raphael recalled one of his several aunts, who had married a Christian, remarking to his mother that she didn't think it possible to be a Jew and to be a lady. "And my mother said: 'Oh, but you're quite a lady, Minnie.' And she said: 'I wasn't until I became a Christian.' So they were dotty. They didn't want to be Jews. They used to sit in the Grand Hotel in Eastbourne, my grandmother's sisters, and when a Jew came in Minnie would say 'Fish!', which is a code word."

I wondered why Jews seem to flock to Eastbourne of all places. I remembered that Howard Jacobson goes there every year with his wife and her mother.

Raphael believes it's a way of acting as English as possible. "We thought that's what the English were like," he said. "They had big flats. They had maids who wheeled in trolleys with chafing dishes with scones and you had to have the bread and butter before you had the bread and butter with jam, then you could have the scone and then you could have the plain cake and then you could have a piece of fruit cake. All of these things in order. So England was a place to me filled with an extraordinary kind of ladders which you could get wrong. And, in a way, it still is."

And that, he thinks, is a difference between the experience of Jews, the outsiders, in England and in America. "There are two million Jews in New York and they could as it were take care of themselves." Not entirely, though. "Being Jewish was always a fairly difficult thing to be and the old stuff about having to work twice as hard to get half as far kicked in there as well. England, though, was different because it was part of the whole fibre of contempt with which the English regard each other all the time. It wasn't visited specifically on Jews although in this specific case that's what I noticed. That's what we do, isn't it? It's the pin on my chair that I feel, not the pin on yours."

What made the difference was Israel. "Whatever anyone may think of the state of Israel, no Jew born after 1948 had any idea what it felt like to be a Jew in New York and in London in the 1930s."

But once that homeland had been established, Jews felt protected. Raphael recalled his time at school when he was subject to continuous anti-Semitic bullying. That was the time "when the Zionists, rightly or wrongly, were seeking to find somewhere in the world where the survivors of the Holocaust could go." It was a time "when it would have suited the British if Hitler had killed all of the Jews in Europe and then none of them would've leaked into the Middle East, they certainly wouldn't have leaked into England."

Israel provided a buffer against such crass anti-Semitism. And this defined Raphael's attitude. He may not always endorse what the Israelis have done and are doing, but he entirely supports the right of the country to exist and sees its very existence as a protection against anti-Semitism.

Howard Jacobson: "Comedy is a serious business."

This view is held, possibly with even more fervour, by Howard Jacobson, who has repeatedly and publicly defended and supported Israel despite his reservations about some of that country's more draconian actions.

In his novel *The Finkler Question* he mercilessly parodies a group of Jewish anti-Zionists who call themselves ASHamed. They meet, perhaps with a parodic inevitability, in the Groucho Club in London, where they discuss how much they deplore Israel's actions, the lack of human rights for Palestinians. Was he suggesting that these Jews who were prepared to criticise Israel, its policies in Gaza and the expansion of home-building on the West Bank, were guilty of anti-Semitism: were self-hating Jews?

"I do detect some anti-Semitism coming from Jews and from non-Jews in certain criticism of Israel," he agreed. "I'm absolutely clear in my own mind that I do not answer to that parody position of somebody who thinks, 'Ah-ah, criticism of Israel, an anti-Semite.' I don't for one moment think that. But I have to give an account of why the anti-Israeli rhetoric is sometimes what it is, is sometimes as vehement as it is, is sometimes as inordinate as it is. Why have some people rushed so quickly to call Israel a Nazi state? Of all the language you could choose. If you want to say it is barbaric, you could say it's worse than Attila the Hun, you could say it's worse than the Romans. Why would you choose 'Nazi'? How can my ears, as a Jew, not prick to that? Why would you choose to insult a Jewish project with an accusation reminding Jews of the worst they've ever suffered?"

This, said Jacobson, was an example of Holocaust aggrandisement. "The Holocaust, we grant you, was a terrible, terrible thing, so you Jews who went through the Holocaust of all people, you of all people should not behave the way you're now behaving. If I hear anybody say that, I hear anti-Semitism. The Holocaust was a learning experience which the Jews did not properly pass. That's when I hear anti-Semitism."

But did he, in his present life, within literary metropolitan circles, encounter much anti-Semitism? No, it was certainly not like his childhood in Manchester when it was very much present.

He remembered how his father physically challenged Oswald Mosley and knocked him off his horse. But even when he was growing up, he recalled, he and his friends shared a standing joke about Jews who see anti-Semitism everywhere.

"Any intelligent Jew knows that this is a failing of the Jewish people," he said. "We do see anti-Semitism everywhere. Is it good for the Jews? How will it affect the Jews? We know all about that absurdity."

But surely, in the way in which he talks about Israel and in his regular journalism, he does seem at least on occasions to be searching for anti-Semitism in much the way that he dismisses as "absurd" in others?

"I wouldn't be able to swear that I have never been guilty of this," he answered. "But I'd be very surprised if I have. I'm very careful about it. I do not feel that I hear anti-Semitism all the time. I've even written things saying I don't care if people don't like the Jews. There are worse things than people disliking Jews. I often feel that the hatred that's felt towards Israel is in some quarters so pathological in itself that it doesn't matter whether it's about anti-Semitism or not. I almost want to say, 'Forget whether it's anti-Semitic, let's just ask what this pathology itself is about.' To hate one place like this so inordinately, what on earth is it about?"

I wondered how much Frederic Raphael shared the view of Jewish anti-Zionists that Jacobson presents in *The Finkler Question*. Didn't he wish to back away from the view that any expression of anti-Israeli sentiments could be construed as anti-Semitic?

"Well, it's a logical matter," Raphael told me. "Is it possible both to be pro-Jewish and anti-Israel? The answer has to be yes. Of course it is, because the two things are not identical, so that isn't really a gross problem. What I think about the people that Howard was attacking is that they suffer from a remarkable form of Jewish vanity. That is the vanity that says: 'It's all got to be our fault. We must've done something.' And the answer is: 'Yes, you did, you crucified Jesus.'"

Raphael then warmed to his theme: the contradiction inherent in both anti-Semitic accusations and Jewish responses to them. "The crucifixion of Jesus and the fall of Jerusalem are linked because Christian propaganda – which is also, of course, Jewish, by the way – insists that the fall of Jerusalem proves that the Jews were being punished for having killed Jesus."

But, he went on, this assumption goes beyond the prejudices of the Church. "Anti-Semitism as a political activity was in fact a function of the Enlightenment, of the philosophers both in Germany and in France, and therefore it has nothing to do with Christianity. So the Holocaust has nothing to do with Christianity, even though it was firmly backed by the Catholic church and by the Lutheran church."

And, he concluded triumphantly: "So the Jews can claim both to have been entirely evicted from the world and also to be central to it. In other words they are what I call 'the margin that runs down the centre of the page'."

Like Howard Jacobson, Raphael detects a kind of arrogant hypocrisy among some of the more outspoken Jewish critics of Israel, like the anti-Zionist academic Jacqueline Rose. "She can seriously believe that it's all the fault of the Zionists that the Muslims, for instance, are anti-Semitic," he said. "But the Muslims have been anti-Semitic for a very, very long time . . . The Jews were dispossessed in Morocco, they were dispossessed in Algeria, they were dispossessed in Egypt. And none of those things count for Jacqueline Rose compared with the fact that the Jews pinched a lot of territory on the West Bank. Well, I quite agree it's awful . . ."

But, Raphael implied, the occupation of the West Bank, criminal though it may be, simply can't be the whole story and the whole reason for anti-Semitism. So he suspects the stance of those Jews who take an extreme position against Israel. And one of those more vocal critics was Miriam Margolyes.

When her acclaimed one-woman show *Dickens' Women* was staged in London she was taken aback to find a small, angry picket line had formed outside the theatre. It was a collection of outraged Jews, protesting at her views on Israel. "I didn't know it when I was performing because I went into the theatre early and this demonstration was going on outside but it was quite vehement and a member of the audience who was supporting me was actually arrested."

This, she told me, is a difficult area for her, "because I don't want to make things worse, I want to make things better. But what I would say," she went on, "is if you go to the West Bank and to Gaza and you see the effect of the Israeli occupation on the people and the way that the occupation is being carried out, whoever you are, you would be appalled. And this is not good for Israel publicly and privately and it should be stopped. And the only way I can see that we can stop it is if the diaspora, the people not in Israel, bring pressure to bear on the Israeli government and say: 'You can't do this, this is wrong and it is contrary to everything that Jewish people believe about how to treat others.' I think we have already lost the propaganda war and I think we deserved to lose it."

And what exactly did she mean by "we"? "I'm saying 'we' because I have to stand alongside Jewish people, because I am one, so my belief, if you like, is with Jews, with Israelis. I can only speak to them. I can't speak to Arabs or Palestinians – only as an outsider, and it would seem to me perhaps to be impertinent to do so – but I'm a Jew and I want Jews to be good and fine as I believe they always used to be. And Israel is an abomination at the moment."

But how did she respond, I wondered, to the concerns of Howard Jacobson and Frederic Raphael that a criticism of Israel can be taken up by anti-Semitic people, that they can use it as an opportunity to voice anti-Semitic opinions? Can such propaganda attacks upon Israel be used to disguise anti-Semitism?

"Without doubt, they are absolutely right," she said at once. "Of course there are anti-Semites! It's a very real thing, anti-Semitism. I've experienced it, loathsome as it is. But I can't hold back a criticism because it might be used against Jews, generally speaking. I don't accept that. I think if you see something is wrong you have to speak out against it whoever is doing the wrong."

Conversations like these with Raphael and Jacobson and Margolyes did, of course, confirm my assumption that Jewishness was an affiliation, an aspect of identity that could not simply be suspended or laid aside. Neither was it something, like my own Catholicism, that could be outgrown or discarded.

My tendency to compare my own one-time religion with Jewishness had from time to time prompted something close to jealousy. I had no wish to embrace Judaic theology or be bar-mitzvah'd but I found it difficult to beat off the suspicion that Jews somehow contrived to lead a fuller and richer intellectual life.

I confessed to Jacobson that rather like Treslove, the central character in *The Finkler Question*, I'd occasionally wished to become Jewish because, well, because it might make me more interesting, more complex, more productively neurotic. But I also told him that I resented my own wish. Why was it that Jews did seem to have so many attributes, why were they so readily credited with intelligence and scholarship and a wonderful sense of humour? It was, I suggested to Howard, as though he and his fellow Jewish novelists were busy appropriating all the most fascinating human qualities and bestowing them upon the Jews.

Howard told me quietly that I'd missed the point of *The Finkler Question*.

Treslove, he explained, is a foolish idealist. "I don't for one moment suppose that what Treslove thinks about Jewishness is what being Jewish is," he reflected. "Treslove's position is touching but absurd. It's wrong, I think, to read this book, or what I do, as offering this kind of sentimental version of Judaism. I am not a sentimentalist of Judaism."

So what, in that case, defines Jewishness for him? "Well, yes, it's the sense of humour, " he snaps back instantly. "It's something Jews have learned to do. All minority groups evolve a shared sense of humour. It's a philosophical attitude to their own – to their minority-ness. . ."

And for the Jews, it's a defence against persecution.

"Nothing deals with a sense of, you know, terror, a history of persecution, quite like a Jewish joke. I mean, it's a wonderful strategy. You know, it's masochistic: you think you can hurt me? I'll hurt myself more in this joke. I will gain mastery over you, you who are not Jewish. You think you can treat us like this – let me show you who we are."

Someone who has pursued the Jewish joke with more tenacity than most is the American comedian Jackie Mason. When he strode into the New York studio I had the feeling that he hadn't listened too intently when our researcher had been briefing him on the nature of the event. For whereas many of my other guests struck a slightly wary stance on arrival as though they were anticipating a minor surgical intervention, Mason burst into the studio, tossing gags and smart remarks around like a drunken wedding guest dispensing confetti. But then, as he quickly told me, he started making an impression on audiences at the age of 13, at his bar-mitzvah party.

"I was very comfortable performing. Talking. I didn't even feel like it was a special effort for me to face an audience. Usually you assume that a 13-year-old kid is frightened and uncomfortable. Nervous, tense, fearful. You think you'll have to rehearse them for weeks, for months. Nobody had to rehearse me even for a second. I had to rehearse what I had to say but I didn't have to rehearse at all how I would say what I was saying. I didn't give a thought to how I'd deliver the speech. All the things that everybody rehearses so much in a 13-year-old kid. I told them, 'Don't tell me anything about that. I'll take care of it.' And I had that attitude when I was 13, like just as if I was 47."

It sounded as though he was already well on the way to a show-business career at 13 but there was another career beckoning. One that would please the family rather more.

"I became a rabbi because I felt a moral obligation to my father to be a rabbi. My father's dream was that all his four sons would be rabbis. And there was a long heritage in the family of rabbis going back maybe hundreds of years, so it was no alternative but to be a rabbi. It was unthinkable to my father that I wouldn't be a rabbi and I couldn't look at him and disappoint him because it was such a holy thing to him that I really felt he'd be heartbroken. So out of compassion for my father I felt it was my mission, that I just couldn't avoid it. So I became a rabbi and the compromise I made is that I became a rabbi but I acted more like a comedian. As soon as I became a rabbi, I started concentrating on comedy because a serious message is not compromised by being funny with it."

So he put actual jokes in his sermons?

"I used to do a lot of comedy in the sermons. But the comedy I did was very material to the message. It wasn't irrelevant or irreverent comedy. It was very meaningful because it highlighted the point. So they enjoyed the message that much more."

But did he believe the message? That was surely also a pretty important part of the rabbi's role.

"I never believed any of it. I believe in the idea of religion but I never was particularly religious. While I was admonishing them not to eat on Yom Kippur I was sneaking out some place where I could hide under the table with a cup of coffee. While I told them never to look at women because it was a sin of the flesh, a girl would walk by and I would lose my place. So I had different values for them and for me. So I felt hypocritical but I felt I was serving a higher purpose. Which was to please my father. So that was the compromise I felt I was allowed to make. My standard of morality was that compassion for my father was more important than whether I had to be honest about myself."

Anyone who has seen Jackie Mason live on stage knows that he delivers his dialogue with all the power and rapidity of a skilled boxer. It's a relentless barrage of gags and observations. He may have already been a funny guy by the age of 13 but, he told me, he also saw himself as standing in a long line of American Jewish comedians, all of whom, like him, cut their teeth by playing in Jewish holiday resorts in the Catskill Mountains. "If you talked about Danny Kaye or Jerry Lewis or Buddy Hackett or almost every Jewish comedian you could think of, they all came from there."

And while that Jewish audience gave the comedians their first break, and Mason himself acknowledges that debt, he confessed to me that his favourite audiences are English. "Because over there not only do they respect a performer more than here," he explained, "but they divorce themselves from the idea of competing with the performer. They see you as a person in another world and they look at you as a person in another business. They don't think that they also are actors. Like every Jew, deep in his heart, thinks that he should have been on the stage."

And this, he explained, is a defining characteristic of Jewishness. Even the Jews who are normal are not exactly normal. "The truth of the matter is that there's no such thing as a normal Jew. It's no accident that the Jews get further in life than almost any other denomination. It's because they're always competing and trying to prove themselves. They're always trying to accomplish something more than the next person."

But, he suggested, it's also the reason why they're so jealous and bitter and "a little obnoxious". On stage he puts it like this:

"They can't say hello without telling me how they look better than me and they want my autograph but it's not for themselves. Every time they give you a compliment they have to take it back. I have a classic thing that happened to me. A woman sits next to me and tells me how good I look. I said, 'Do I really look that good?' She said, 'You look very good.' I said 'No kidding? I didn't know I looked that good.' She said, 'I didn't say you looked *that* good.'"

Afterword

"We can map the precise moment a public figure becomes a celebrity," writes Graeme Turner in *Understanding Celebrity*. "It occurs at the point at which media interest in their activities is transferred from reporting on their public role . . . to investigating the details of their private lives."

So it's hardly surprising that many of my *In Confidence* guests have had to find ways to deal with such intrusion. Some confessed to enjoying, even exploiting this aspect of their fame. But others have resisted such probing, or unwillingly endured it.

The whole cult of celebrity disgusts Jonathan Miller, who feels that TV has been reduced to something vulgar, something that lacks what he called intellectual finesse. "It's part and parcel of this – this much more widespread obsession with fame and celebrity," he told me. And our politicians are as vulnerable as anyone to this decaying of intellectual rigour. Both David Cameron and Tony Blair, he said, "are infected, particularly Blair, with – with this HIV of celebrity."

Others, though, positively embrace their fame and status. Stephen Fry even sees it as an advantage. Talking about his documentaries on the subject of manic depression, and his own experience of it, Stephen Fry said his celebrity allowed him to legitimise a condition that is too often stigmatised. "And if there's one thing that fame gives you that is good – ultimately really good, it is that you are, essentially, immune from that kind of stigma."

But of all the people I've talked to over these five series of *In Confidence*, one really does epitomise the extreme end of the celebrity spectrum. Uri Geller has created an image of himself so complete, so overriding, that it's almost as if he's turned himself into a brand. So when I suggested that the one gimmick that sparked his career, the ability to bend spoons, didn't appear to have much practical value, he was quick to correct me.

"You see, Laurie," he explained, "the fame around Uri Geller that started with the trivial spoon-bending came to a peak from which I could transfer myself into the realms of pure motivational lectures. And it's fascinating to see the spoon-bending became the placebo effect . . . because, hey, I will be remembered for – for the spoon-bending. You see, there was nothing like it before Uri Geller was born. Wow, unbelievable!"

Uri Geller, in short, has bought his own myth to the point where he has somehow been separated from reality.

So how do other very successful people manage to avoid this trap?

Lily Allen seems able to separate herself completely from her public image – even laughing at its absurdity. David Schwimmer says he has escaped from the damaging temptations of celebrity because fame came to him relatively late.

"I got *Friends* when I was 27 years old so I was already an adult. I had very healthy friendships in my life, my theatre company, my parents, my family – so I was on steady ground. That was a very good foundation. What I'm saying is that a young person, someone like Justin Bieber or anyone who becomes very successful at a very young age, I feel for them because it's gonna be a lot harder."

Such strategies may vary, but time and again in these interviews one overriding answer kept resounding: work, work and more work. Whoever was most wedded to their work, the achievements that gave them celebrity in the first place, was most likely to escape its worst excesses.

No one represents this simple equation more eloquently than Alan Ayckbourn, who, after 50 years and almost as many plays, continues to live in Scarborough and to direct his work there. But if even that commitment to work doesn't vanquish the worst effect of celebrity, there's always a local to provide a blast of reality.

Alan, it seems, had been taking a morning walk along the South Cliff promenade in his home town of Scarborough when he was stopped by an elderly Yorkshireman who, despite the mildness of the day, was wearing the regulation overcoat, muffler and flat cap.

"Excuse me," he said. "But aren't you Alan Ayckbourn?"

"Indeed," said Alan politely.

"And you write them plays, don't you, Alan?"

Alan nodded.

"And you've got a play on right now at the Scarborough Theatre. And you've got plays on in London as well?"

"That's right," said Alan.

"And they've made a couple of films from your plays, haven't they, Alan?"

"Indeed they have."

"You must have a lot of brass, Alan!"

A smile from Alan.

"So can I ask you a question, Alan?"

"I rather thought you already had."

"If you've got all that brass, Alan," said the Yorkshireman in a deeply suspicious tone of voice, "why don't you live in Bridlington?"

zero
books

Contemporary culture has eliminated both the concept of the public and the figure of the intellectual. Former public spaces – both physical and cultural – are now either derelict or colonized by advertising. A cretinous anti-intellectualism presides, cheerled by expensively educated hacks in the pay of multinational corporations who reassure their bored readers that there is no need to rouse themselves from their interpassive stupor. The informal censorship internalized and propagated by the cultural workers of late capitalism generates a banal conformity that the propaganda chiefs of Stalinism could only ever have dreamt of imposing. Zer0 Books knows that another kind of discourse – intellectual without being academic, popular without being populist – is not only possible: it is already flourishing, in the regions beyond the striplit malls of so-called mass media and the neurotically bureaucratic halls of the academy. Zer0 is committed to the idea of publishing as a making public of the intellectual. It is convinced that in the unthinking, blandly consensual culture in which we live, critical and engaged theoretical reflection is more important than ever before.